Boosting Skills for Greener Jobs in Flanders, Belgium

Please cite this publication as:
OECD (2017), *Boosting Skills for Greener Jobs in Flanders, Belgium*, OECD Publishing, Paris.
http://dx.doi.org/10.1787/9789264265264-en

ISBN 978-92-64-26525-7 (print)
ISBN 978-92-64-26526-4 (online)
ISBN 978-92-64-26895-1 (epub)

Series: OECD Green Growth Studies
ISSN 2222-9515 (print)
ISSN 2222-9523 (online)

Photo credits: Cover © design by advitam for the OECD.

Corrigenda to OECD publications may be found on line at: *www.oecd.org/publishing/corrigenda*.

Acknowledgements

This report was prepared by Nathalie Cliquot (Policy Analyst) under the supervision of Francesca Froy, Jonathan Barr and Sylvain Giguère (Head of Division) with support from Michela Meghnagi and Nikolett Kis.

Sections of the report were drafted by members of an expert team composed by Nathalie Cliquot (OECD), Mr Kris Bachus, Ms. Lize Van Dyck (KU Leuven), Prof. Philip Cooke (Centre for Innovation, Bergen University College, Norway), Francesca Froy (OECD), Michela Meghnagi (OECD), Angela Attrey (OECD), and Jonathan Barr (OECD).

This project would not have been possible without the participation and co-operation from the Departments of Work and Social Economy and Environment, Nature, and Energy of the Flemish Government, Ghent City, Vlakwa, Antwerp province and the West Flanders province. In particular, the city of Ghent and the provinces of West Flanders and Antwerp hosted the project local roundtables in October 2014, while WSE hosted the final workshop in Ghent in December 2014.

The project and report benefitted from the active contribution from a steering committee, including:

- Ann Van den Cruyce and Raf Boey, from the Department for Work and Social Economy (WSE)
- Jan Kielemoes and Annemie Janssens from the Environment, Nature and Energy Department (LNE)
- Dirk Van der Stede and Dirk Halet from the Flanders Knowledge Centre for Water (Vlakwa)
- Fanny Mestdagh, Alien Vanhee and Barbara Govaert from Ghent City
- Myriam Rebahi and Gitte Devries, from the province of Antwerp
- Ann Overmeire and Heidi Hanssens from the province of West Flanders

Finally, Johan Person from the company Tell ID2 contributed to the delivery of the company survey in Flanders in October 2014 and Irena Kondratenko assisted the expert team to animate local roundtables. Barbara Cachova (OECD, LEED) also assisted the authors with layout and formatting.

Table of contents

Tables

Figures

Follow OECD Publications on:

 http://twitter.com/OECD_Pubs

 http://www.facebook.com/OECDPublications

 http://www.linkedin.com/groups/OECD-Publications-4645871

 http://www.youtube.com/oecdilibrary

http://www.oecd.org/oecddirect/

Executive summary

The transition to a low-carbon, resource efficient and green economy can only be made by developing the right skills, knowledge and competencies. Such skills can be defined as "the knowledge, abilities, values and attitudes needed to live in, develop and support a sustainable and resource-efficient society". In countries that rely on energy- and emissions intensive activities, the transition towards a green economy might induce severe adjustment costs, both economically and socially. The structural economic changes required for the shift to a green economy will necessitate careful planning and effective implementation at the local level.

This OECD project aims to analyse the skills dimension of the transition to the green economy at the local level. In particular, it aims to explore how selected local areas/ industry clusters identify the specific skills needed to support green growth, and how related skills policies and practices can be made more effective in supporting and accelerating the transition to a green economy.

In Flanders (Belgium), the study has focused on the agro-food, construction and chemicals sectors, which are important for the local economies of several Flemish provinces. For these sectors, an in-depth review was undertaken, which included semi-directed interviews with business federations and individual companies as well as a phone survey on company practices.

Measuring the transition towards a green economy at the local level in Flanders

The OECD Green Growth strategy has identified a number of indicators that help countries measure their progress towards a greener economy. This OECD project proposes a method for adapting this strategy to the regional and local level. This is important because measuring the transition towards a green economy and providing benchmarks can stimulate local authorities to take action based on evidence and a shared understanding of the challenges. For Flanders, the choice of benchmark regions was based on the regions and countries selected for the Flanders Outlook 2014 (Government of Flanders, 2014). The benchmark regions are considered solid performers in terms of levels of education, R&D and innovation as well as employment in knowledge intensive and creative sectors.

With a well-educated population and a relative low unemployment rate, Flanders is well placed for the transition to a green economy. Flanders performs well compared to other jurisdictions on many environment activities, including those that apply to waste management. However, Flanders could improve its performance on activities related to air pollution and CO_2 emissions, especially from the transportation sector. In particular, Flanders is in the middle of the distribution when measuring investments in R&D and patents applications, far below the German regions of Bavaria and Baden Württemberg.

Flanders recognises the strategic importance of greening skills and jobs and fostering green innovation. Introduced in 2009, the Flanders in Action strategy paved the way for improved policy co-ordination on 13 transversal societal challenges, with several themes related to the transition to a green economy. Education and training agencies such as VDAB (e.g. the Flemish public employment service), Syntra Flanders (Flemish Agency for Entrepreneurial Training) and AHOVOKS (Flemish Agency for higher education, adult education, qualifications and grants) have integrated green elements in their activities. The new Flanders Innovation policy is likely to reinforce the focus on smart specialisation and business clusters. This can be seen as an opportunity to better identify potential skill needs and gaps in selected clusters and tailor the response of education and training providers.

Flanders is well integrated in international networks and is involved in a number of initiatives such as the Vanguard project on smart specialisation. Furthermore, Flemish universities and research centres participate in the European Knowledge and Innovation Communities (KIC). In addition, many knowledge-sharing platforms between the business and education sector exist although the green focus is not always prominent (e.g. for the food cluster in West Flanders). Stakeholders are not always aware of many of the interesting initiatives that have been introduced and the multiplication of initiatives could undermine business participation, as it may be difficult to identify where resources are best placed.

The construction, chemicals and agro-food sectors are transitioning to a greener economy at a difference pace in Flanders. In the construction sector, a stable and predictable regulatory framework has helped to identify skills needs and gaps and the education and training system has adapted its response to companies' needs. The chemicals industry has started to recognise the importance of sustainability in the training of workers but has difficulties finding the highly technical and multidisciplinary skills required. Collaboration between the sector and the education and training system is mainly focused on building a talent pipeline. The agro-food sector has limited awareness of the green economy transition. It is currently not anticipating major changes related to skills for greening its practices.

The majority of Flemish companies interviewed for this study have taken steps to green their business especially in relation to waste management and energy efficiency. Few claimed to have completely reshaped their business. Companies pointed to a number of strategies taken to transition to the green economy, including:

- *Building a talent pipeline* which ensures that the education and training sector prepares individuals with appropriate skills. Activities include collaboration with the secondary and postsecondary education sector and support for traineeships.
- *Recruitment*, such as sending job vacancies to universities or associated faculty.
- *Training* by establishing linkages with the sector federations, hiring specialised consultants to train employees, and establishing mentors within the company.
- *Knowledge sharing networks* which encourage employee participation in thematic conferences, collaboration with other companies in the sector, or with companies in the value chain.

The green transition is having an impact on skills and occupational profiles, and firms signalled that there is an increasing need for technical skills. In order to have the skills necessary to green businesses, more than half of the firms had to upskill or retrain current staff, while a third needed to hire external consultants. Training is considered costly and the timing of training courses does not always suit business needs. The public sector is expected to assist firms in meeting the emerging skill needs. Knowledge-sharing activities such as business clusters or supply-chain platforms could be a useful tool to assist firms in greening their business.

Foreword

The Local Economic and Employment Development (LEED) programme of the Organisation for Economic Co-operation and Development (OECD) is implementing a research project on "Boosting skills ecosystems for greener jobs", with the support of the European Commission.

The project builds on previous projects on "Greening jobs and skills: Labour market implications of addressing climate change" (2009-10) and "Measuring the potential of green growth: Indicators of local transition to a low-carbon economy"(2011-12). The project considers green growth and the green economy in a broad sense, not only focusing on climate change and low-carbon aspects. This follows the OECD definition of green growth policies as policies "that favour the transition to a low-carbon, resource efficient economy, that improve the management of the natural asset base, that raise the environmental quality of life, and that create opportunities associated with changes of production and consumption" (OECD, 2013).

The "Boosting skills ecosystems for greener jobs" project aims to analyse the skills dimension of the transition to a green economy at the local level. In particular, it aims to explore how selected local areas/industry clusters identify the specific skills needed to support green growth, and how related skills policies and practices can be made more effective in supporting and accelerating the transition to a green economy. Because a mixture of transversal and specific skills is needed by different industry sectors, the project investigated how flexible and responsive the education and labour market system is to developing these skills to meet business objectives, both now and in the future.

The methodology addresses the following key questions:

- *Which skills are needed for accelerating the job and entrepreneurship potential of green industry clusters and supporting the development of the blue economy? Which strategies can be proposed for strengthening green skills ecosystems?*
- *Which skills are needed for greening high-energy/carbon-intensive industry clusters? Which strategies can be proposed to support the transformation of industries and foster the jobs of the future?*
- *What is the role of education and labour market institutions, actors and research institutions? What role for the private sector? In particular, it is important to understand:*
  - *The flexibility and responsiveness of the education, training and labour market system to current green skills gaps;*
  - *The degree to which the education, training and labour market system is anticipating and supporting future change in industry practices associated with green growth;*
  - *The degree to which knowledge sharing networks and activities are helping to accelerate the transition to green growth and the extent to which public policy makers could further facilitate such exchanges.*

A variety of places and sectors have been analysed including carbon intensive industries, eco-industries and the special case of coastal regions. Coastal regions are significant because the emerging "blue economy", namely the sustainable development of the marine and maritime sectors in industries including aquaculture, blue energy, tourism and deep sea minerals, can be an engine of local growth. In Flanders (Belgium) the study focused on the agro-food, construction and chemicals sectors, which are important sectors for the local economies of several Flemish provinces.

Company surveys were carried out to identify the extent to which businesses are greening their practices, products and services and the related impact on skills and jobs. In all case studies, companies were contacted by phone. It should be highlighted that this methodology approach has potential limitations. The questionnaire included references to the green economy; therefore, there is a risk of potential bias in the survey with responses more likely to come from companies with an existing interest in the green economy. Given these noted limitations, the survey nevertheless provides interesting and useful insights into business perceptions.

Survey results were complemented by interviews with selected firms and stakeholders. Seven roundtables and events were organised with stakeholders (public authorities, public employment services, universities, industry representatives) between October 2014-April 2015 to refine desk research and survey conclusions. In Flanders, a series of local roundtables were organised in Antwerp, Ghent and Roeselare from the 1-3 October 2014 to collect additional stakeholder views. A final workshop was organised in Ghent on the 3rd of December to refine the research findings and policy recommendations.

Chapter 1

Green skills and the transition to a green economy

While much attention has been paid to the need to transition to a green economy, there has been relatively less policy focus on the need to build the skills in the labour force to facilitate this shift. This chapter outlines the case for green skills and the impact of transitioning to sustainable production on local labour markets, with particular reference to Flanders, Belgium.

The transition to a low-carbon, resource-efficient and green economy can only be made by developing the right skills, knowledge and competences. Such skills can be defined broadly as "the knowledge, abilities, values and attitudes needed to live in, develop and support a sustainable and resource-efficient society (Cedefop, 2012) or "skills needed by the workforce, in all sectors and at all levels, in order to help the adaptation of products, services and processes to the changes due to climate change and to environmental requirements and regulations" (OECD 2014a).

The green economy can be defined as an economy that aims to reduce environmental and ecological impacts, while promoting sustainable growth. It is expected that the green economy will lead to a "progressive redefinition of skills requirements in many jobs," across many sectors (ICF GHK, 2011: 3). The biggest changes are to be expected in changing skills in traditional and existing occupations. All jobs are expected to become increasingly greener. A study by the International Labour Organisation (ILO) shows that a lack of skills will pose a major barrier in the transition towards green economies and the creation of green jobs (ILO, 2011).

Several skills can be considered green, and play a role in the transition towards sustainable consumption and production systems. An OECD-LEED study concluded that "skills to support innovation and adaptability will be as important as technical skills, as industries will gradually adapt to the need to better harness and dispose of resources" (OECD, 2014b). This means that both transversal and industry-specific (and technical) skills will be needed. With regard to transversal skills, four main categories can be observed. First of all, technological skills will be required (e.g. in research or engineering). Secondly, management skills and knowledge on techniques are needed, (e.g. to become more energy efficient, reduce waste generation and pollution). Third, skills on innovation and management for change, particularly communication skills, are needed. Finally, "transversal generic skills" are necessary, which should support the overall transition of workers in different industries (OECD, 2014b).

The current shortage of relevant skills identified by the ILO can be attributed to a multitude of factors: an underestimation of the growth of certain green sectors (e.g. energy efficiency in building), an overall shortage of scientists and engineers, a low attractiveness of certain sectors (e.g. waste management) and the general structure per country to facilitate skills creation (e.g. a lack of teaching) (ILO, 2011).

The ILO also found that many public policies are inadequate in addressing the skills component of adaptation and mitigation policies (ILO, 2011). According to the OECD, several policy responses to enhance skill development and a transition towards a green economy can be distinguished. First, public policy co-ordination can be optimised. Second, "portable" skills (which can be transferred from one job to another) and lifelong learning should be fostered (OECD, 2013). Third, market developments should be matched to regulatory activity. Fourth, transparency around policy action should be enhanced. Fifth, strategic capacity should be developed within SMEs, and finally, investments in R&D for anticipating and addressing knowledge gaps should be enhanced (OECD, 2014b).

The European Union is becoming increasingly active in the field of green jobs and green skills. Linked to the target to increase the EU's employment rate to 75 per cent, the "Agenda for New Skills and Jobs" recognises the need for skills to play a key role in the transition towards a green economy. The importance of the green economy transition is also recognised through the EU's economic governance mechanisms such as the European Semester, a mechanism established in 2010 to better co-ordinate economic policies in European Union countries. In 2013 and 2014, the Annual Growth Survey, which serves as a basis for the European semester review and contains priorities for national reform programmes, highlighted the importance of long term investments in education, research, innovation, energy and climate action and resource efficiency. In this context, "integrating more people into the labour market through green job creation", "using the potential of waste and water management to generate new jobs" and "addressing skills gaps which prevent innovation" are described as major opportunities (European Union, 2010a). The EU's Growth Strategy until 2020 specifically notes that future growth mechanisms are expected to be sustainable in order to meet ambitious targets for emissions reduction and energy use and efficiency. This will be accomplished through a new industrial policy that aims to support businesses, especially small businesses, to the shift to a low-carbon economy (European Commission, 2010b). In July 2014, the EU adopted an initiative on green employment, estimating that a one percent increase in the growth of the water industry could create between 10 000 and 20 000 jobs (see Box 1.1).

The potential of the green economy to create new jobs in the long run can be directly or indirectly achieved through supply chains (ILO, 2011). The challenge for environmental policy is thus to choose policies that aim to both integrate environmental awareness and maximise productive and decent working standards (ILO 2011).

The transition towards a green economy and adjacent skills development will not happen instantly: it requires training and education organisations to work together with local actors through an integrated approach (OECD, 2014b). Existing jobs will change due to this greener economy, which will require adjustments to the current training, education and qualifications system. The role of the private sector and of public-private collaboration will also be critical. The emergence of industry platforms can help create co-operation between firms and across sectors (OECD, 2014b). Universities and vocational training institutions can partner with businesses to develop knowledge-sharing platforms to promote innovation at the local level and allow firms to reduce training costs (OECD, 2014b).

The transition to a green economy will have an effect on the labour market. Some experts fear that a transition to a green economy will lead to lower productivity, extra costs for producers and overall lower economic development. Other experts stress the importance of technological and process innovation, which should be an economic boost to local economies and industries (OECD, 2014b). However, if the transition towards a green, circular and low-carbon economy is to be made, skills development is important and necessary for workers to be able to transition from traditional "brown" industries to new, greener industries (OECD, 2014b). However, the creation of green jobs will not necessarily result in automatic replacement of existing employment in so-called "brown" industries: the new jobs which will be created may not necessarily go to the people who will lose their jobs due to a phase-out of these "brown" industries (ILO, 2011).

Most experts agree that the effect will largely be concentrated on two types of sectors. First, carbon-intensive industries, such as the agricultural, petroleum or chemical

Box 1.1. **The European Union Green Employment initiative**

The EU s green employment initiative estimates that 400 000 new jobs could be created by improving waste prevention and management and another 400 000 jobs by making buildings more energy efficient and implementing the requirements of the energy efficiency directive. A one percent increase in the growth of the water industry could create between 10 000 and 20 000 jobs.

The initiative calls for actions to:

- Bridge existing skills gaps by fostering skills developments and better forecasting skills needs across sectors and industries;
- Anticipate change and secure transitions by: assessing and developing sector initiatives on anticipating and managing restructuring; supporting peer reviews on adequate labour market policies; working with the European Public Employment Services Network to support occupational mobility to meet specific labour market needs in the green economy;
- Boosting job creation by making efficient use of EU funding; by shifting taxes away from labour towards pollution; promoting green public procurement; entrepreneurship and social enterprises;
- Increase data quality and monitoring of labour market developments by providing support to national statistical offices through financial and training support; building on the framework of employment and environment indicators developed by the EU Employment Committee to support monitoring of policies in the context of the Europe 2020 Strategy and the European Semester;
- Promoting social dialogue at cross industry and sector levels as a pre-requisite to facilitate the greening of the economy. As recommended by the European Resource Efficiency Platform (EREP), the Commission will support workers' involvement in matters related to environmental management, energy and resource use and emerging risks at the work place, enhance workers' rights to information and consultation, and develop sector-wide resource efficiency roadmaps; and
- Strengthening international co-operation.

Source: European Commission (2014).

industries will experience the most significant changes. Second, the creation of new greener industries and drivers of eco-innovation will have a significant impact on the labour market as well, especially through the creation of new jobs in renewable energy (OECD, 2014b).

However, it remains difficult to fully estimate and quantify to the evolution of the green economy and green jobs (OECD, 2014b). Projections of the amount of new jobs that can be expected are scarce. Green growth is not expected to create a large number of new jobs (OECD 2014b). However, in countries which have an energy- and emissions-intensive economy, the transition towards a green economy might induce severe adjustment costs, both economically and socially. An example of this can be seen through the downsizing and restructuring of emission-intensive industries.

However, this transition will also foster growth in green sectors. In Flanders, there have been attempts to quantify the amount of new jobs that will be created in the green economy. Dubois and Christis (2014) estimate that 27 000 new jobs would be created in the waste management, recycling and the circular economy sectors in Flanders. Recent work from the OECD (2012) notes that 2 000 000 jobs across Europe could be created if the EU is successful in meeting its target to attain 20% of total energy consumption from renewables.

Flanders has also articulated a number of policy priorities (which are further highlighted in Chapter 3 of this report), which will contribute to a smoother transition to the green economy. These include the Smart Specialisation Policy of Flanders, which aims to encourage the 'bottom-up development of new value chains' in seven key strategic clusters: sustainable chemistry, specialised manufacturing solutions, personalised cure and care, value-added logistics, specialised agro-food, sustainable energy use in housing, and information communications technology. (Department of Economy. Science and Innovation, 2014) There are also a number of local reform projects being undertaken in reference to the particular industrial concentration of the municipality, such as the agro-food industry in West Flanders and the diamond industry in Antwerp.

References

Arbeid & Milieu (2010), *Green jobs, http://groenejobs.be/uploads/Documenten/am_2010_3_katern.pdf* (accessed 18 December 2014).

Cedefop (2012), *Green skills and environmental awareness in vocational education and training,* European Commission, Luxembourg.

Department of Economy, Science and Innovation (2014), *The Strategic Policy Framework for Smart Specialisation in Flanders*, Policy Note Rev. 12/2014.

Dubois, M. And M. Christis (2014), *Verkennende analyse van het economisch belang van afvalbeheer, recyclage en de circulaire economie in Vlaanderen,* Steunpunt Duurzaam Materialenbeheer, Leuven.

European Commission (2014) *Employment: Commission presents Green Employment Initiative to support structural shift to green growth by maximizing job opportunities*, European Commission, *http://europa.eu/rapid/press-release_MEMO-14-446_fr.htm.*

European Commission (2013), *Draft Join Employment Report, Communication from the Commission on Annual Growth Survey, http://ec.europa.eu/europe2020/pdf/2014/jer2014_en.pdf* (accessed 20 October 2015).

European Commission (2013), *Promoting green jobs through the crisis: A handbook of best practices in Europe,* European Commission, Directorate-General for Employment, Social Affairs and inclusion.

European Commission (2010a), *Greening the European Semester*. European Commission, *http://ec.europa.eu/environment/integration/green_semester/index_en.htm.*

European Commission (2010b), *Europe 2020 in a Nutshell, http://ec.europa.eu/europe2020/europe-2020-in-a-nutshell/priorities/sustainable-growth/index_en.htm* (accessed 16 February 2016).

ICF GHK (2011), *Skills needs in greening economies.*

IDEA Consult (2011), *Gevolgen van het klimaatbeleid voor de Vlaamse arbeidsmarkt.*

ILO (2011), *Skills for green jobs a global view,* International Labour Organisation.

OECD (2014b), *Job Creation and Local Economic Development*, OECD Publishing, Paris, *http://dx.doi.org/10.1787/9789264215009-en.*

OECD (2013), "Greener Skills and Jobs for a Low-Carbon Future", *OECD Green Growth Papers*, No. 2013/10, OECD Publishing, Paris, *http://dx.doi.org/10.1787/5k3v1dtzlxzq-en.*

OECD (2014a), *Greener Skills and Jobs*, OECD Green Growth Studies, OECD Publishing, Paris, *http://dx.doi.org/10.1787/9789264208704-en.*

OECD (2012), "The Jobs Potential of a Shift Towards a Low-Carbon Economy", *OECD Green Growth Papers*, No. 2012/01, OECD Publishing, Paris, *http://dx.doi.org/10.1787/5k9h3630320v-en.*

Chapter 2

Flanders and the transition to a green economy in the OECD green growth framework

This chapter examines Flanders' capacity to transition to a green economy using the framework of the OECD's Green Growth Indicators. It analyses the socio-economic context and the resources, asset base, labour market situation in both the Flemish region and in Belgium, and benchmarks these indicators to European counterparts.

The OECD Green Growth strategy

Green growth means fostering economic growth and development while ensuring that natural assets continue to provide the resources and environmental services on which our well-being relies. To do this, it must catalyse investment and innovation that will underpin sustained growth and give rise to new economic opportunities (OECD, 2011). Reflecting on the cross-cutting nature of green growth, the OECD Green Growth strategy was formally launched in June 2009 to bring economic, environmental, social, technological and development aspects together into a comprehensive analytical framework.

As part of this strategy, an indicator framework was established to track progress towards green growth at the national level. A first set of indicators was proposed in *Towards Green Growth: Monitoring Progress* in 2011 and updated in *Green Growth Indicators* in 2014. Since then, indicators have evolved as new comparable data have become available.

Relevant data are currently grouped under the following five thematic areas. Figure 2.1 below shows more in detail the indicators under each thematic area.

Figure 2.1. **OECD Green Growth strategy indicators**

	Socio-economic context and characteristics of growth	• Economic growth and structure • Productivity and trade • Labour markets, education and income • Socio-demographic patterns
1	The environmental and resource productivity of the economy	• Carbon and energy productivity • Resource productivity: materials, nutrients, water • Multi-factor productivity
2	The natural asset base	• Renewable stocks: water, forest, fish resources • Non-renewable stocks: mineral resources • Biodiversity and ecosystems
3	The environmental dimension of quality of life	• Environmental health and risks • Environmental services and amenities
4	Economic opportunities and policy responses	• Technology and innovation • Environmental goods and services • International financial flows • Prices and transfers • Skills and training • Regulations and management approaches

Measuring the transition towards a green economy at the local level in Flanders

Measuring the transition towards a green economy and providing benchmarks can stimulate local authorities to take action. The OECD LEED research project "*Indicators of local transition to a low-carbon economy*" therefore proposed an approach to adapt the OECD Green Growth national framework to the local level. The issues related to data availability and timeliness appeared to be even stronger when working at the sub-national level which is the case for Flanders.

Finding a suitable benchmark is also crucial. The OECD Green Growth strategy compares the performance of each country with the OECD average according to certain established indicators (see Figure 2.1). For the regional or sub-regional level, the approach and the relevant indicators need to be adjusted to the local dimension. In particular, it can be relevant to compare the performance of a local area with areas of similar socio-economic characteristics or which are considered frontrunners in the transition towards a green economy rather than with the OECD average. For Flanders, the choice of benchmark regions was based on the regions and countries selected for the Flanders Outlook 2014 (Government of Flanders, 2014). The benchmark regions are considered good performers in terms of the following indicators: levels of education and lifelong learning, R&D and innovation as well as employment in knowledge intensive and creative sectors. For international comparisons, this chapter benchmarks local areas participating in the project *Boosting Skills for Greener Jobs*. The benchmarking countries/regions for the selected indicators are listed in the table below:

Table 2.1. **Benchmark countries and regions**

Belgium	Flanders
Denmark	
Finland	
France	Midi Pyrenees
Germany	Baden Wurttemberg
	Bayern
Greece	Attica/Athens
Netherlands	Oost Nederland
	West Nederland
	Zuid Nederland
Poland	Pomorskie
Spain	Basque country
Sweden	
United Kingdom	North West England
	East of England
	South East England
	South West England
	Scotland

The choice of the data presented in this chapter is mainly based on relevance in relation to the OECD Green Skills indicators presented in Table 2.1 above and availability at the regional level in order to make reliable comparison across benchmarks. When data was not available for Flanders, Belgium was used instead and compared to the other benchmarking regions used in the Flanders Outlook, to neighbouring countries or to the OECD or EU average. In order to highlight local differences, additional analysis was performed when data existed at a lower level of disaggregation.

The socio-economic context and characteristics of growth

Understanding the socio-economic context and characteristics of growth, including productivity, labour market characteristics and demographic patterns, can help to understand the broader national context. In the following, indicators will be analysed more in detail both for Flanders and Belgium.

Economic growth and structure

Flanders is a wealthy region with a high economic performance. In terms of GDP per capita, in 2011 Flanders was situated in the middle of the distribution when compared to the other benchmarks. However, as many large companies and Flemish public offices are located in Brussels, this result can be misleading. When the data is corrected for commuters and includes people who live in Flanders but work elsewhere, Flanders ranks fifth just after the West of the Netherlands, the Basque Country and the German regions (Government of Flanders, 2014).

Figure 2.2. **GDP per capita, 2011**

Current price, US Dollar

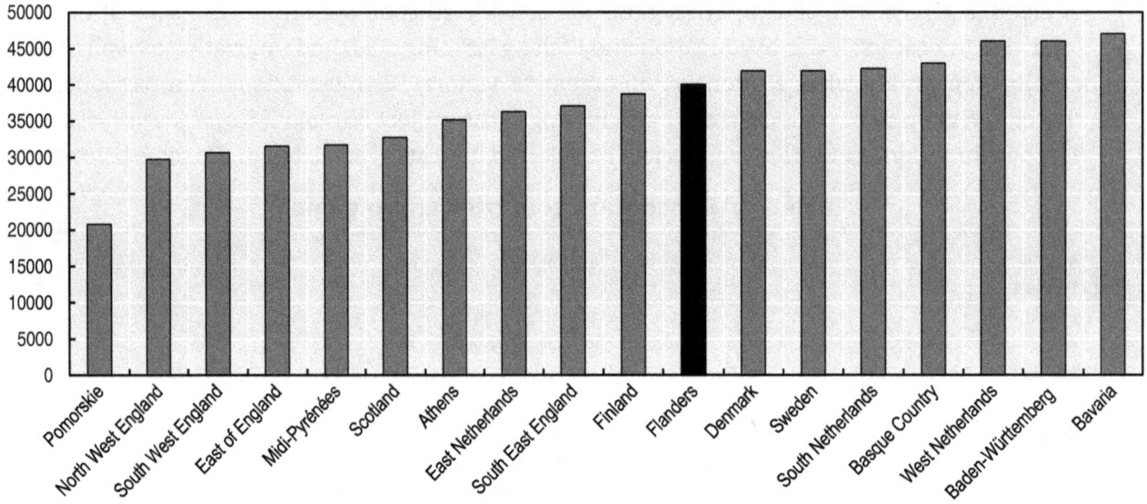

Source: OCDE (2013), « Large regions, TL2: Regional accounts », *OECD Regional Statistics* (base de données), *http://dx.doi.org/10.1787/data-00522-en.*

Productivity and trade

Labour productivity is a driver for economic growth and increased living standards. Figure 2.3 below show labour productivity for Flanders and benchmarking countries and regions measured as regional gross value added from all activities per worker. Flanders has very high levels of labour productivity. Unlike most benchmarking regions, when looking at trends over time, Flanders also shows levels of productivity similar to the pre-crisis period (2007) (Flemish government, 2014).

Labour markets, education and income

The population of Flanders is overall well-educated with 36% of people aged 25-64 having tertiary education attainment in 2013. This is similar to many other benchmarks including Denmark, North-West England and Athens, Greece. In the same year, 7.5% of people aged 18-24 were categorised as "early school leavers" – defined by Eurostat as those in the age group who only have lower secondary education or less and are no longer in education or training. This is one of the lowest levels in Europe and is similar to comparable regions in Sweden, Baden Wurttemberg and Bavaria.

Similar to other benchmark regions and countries, around 70% of the labour force (15-64 years old) in Flanders is employed in the services sector and slightly less than 20% in the manufacturing sector (including energy). As shown in Figure 2.4 below, Flanders shows one of the lowest unemployment rates (5% in 2013) and a relative low youth unemployment rate. Interestingly, after a decrease in unemployment – both total and for youth – in 2011 and 2012, both indicators registered a remarkable increase in 2013.

Figure 2.3. **Labour productivity, 2010**

Constant price, 2005 US Dollar

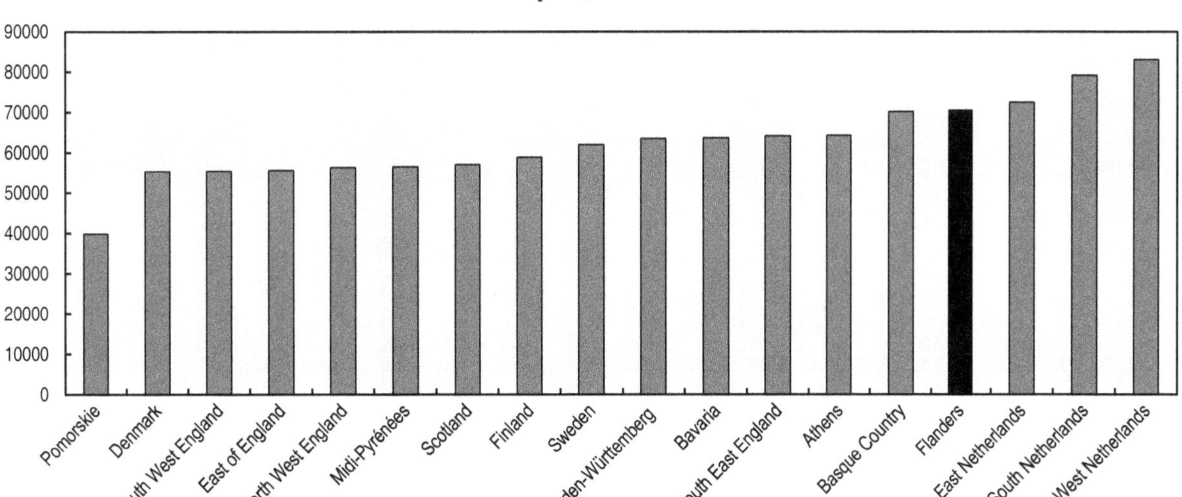

Source: OCDE (2013), "Large regions, TL2: Regional accounts", *OECD Regional Statistics* (base de données), *http://dx.doi.org/10.1787/data-00522-en.*

Figure 2.4. **Unemployment rate and youth unemployment rate, European regions, 2013**

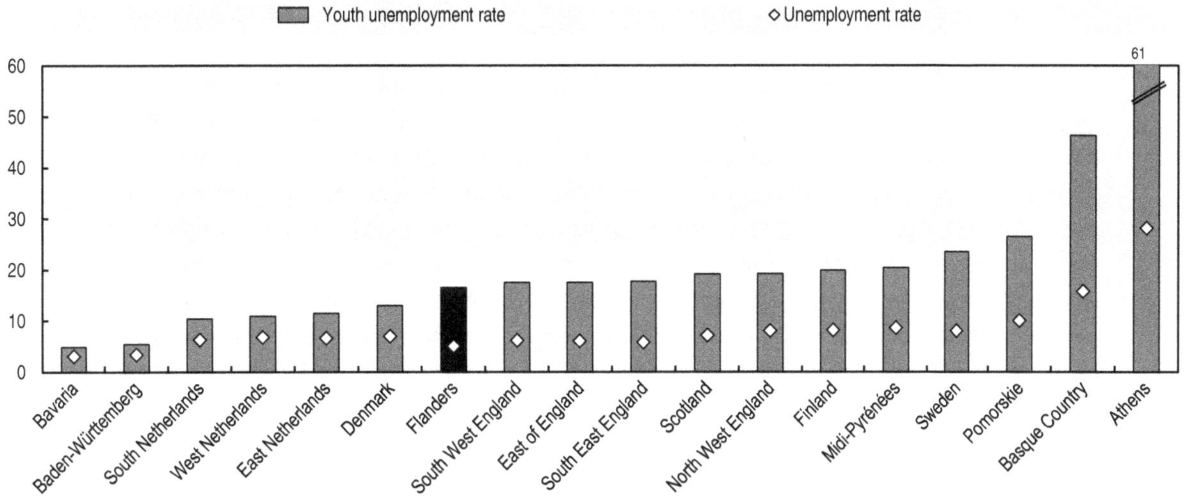

Source: OECD (2011), "Large regions, TL2: Regional labour market", *OECD Regional Statistics* (database), *http://dx.doi.org/10.1787/data-00523-en.*

Socio-demographic patterns

Flanders has a population of approximately 6 300 000 inhabitants, a similar population to both east-England and north-west England. Among the benchmarks, Flanders is around the middle of the distribution (see Figure 2.5). When looking at population change over time, Flanders is the fifth region in terms of average annual growth (6.7%), after three regions in the United Kingdom and Midi-Pyrénées.

Analysis of local data

Flanders is composed of five provinces. The most populous is Antwerp with around 1.8 million inhabitants, followed by East Flanders with 1.44 million inhabitants. The population

Figure 2.5. **Population, European regions, 2012**

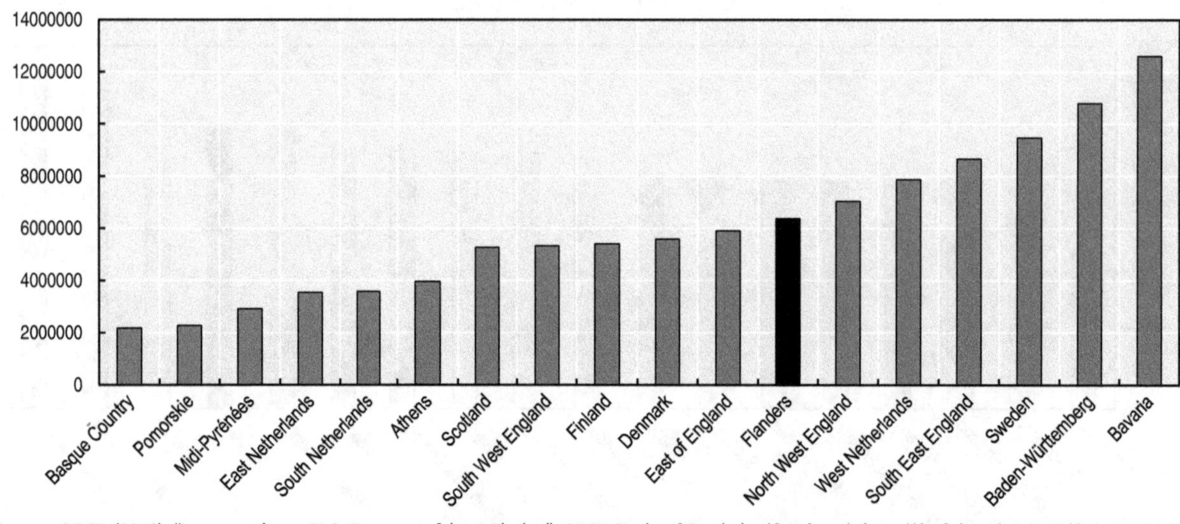

Source: OECD (2013), "Large regions, TL2: Demographic statistics", *OECD Regional Statistics* (database), *http://dx.doi.org/10.1787/data-00520-en.*

structure is very similar across provinces, with around two thirds of the population at working age (15-64).

In 2013, the unemployment rate in Flanders was around 5%. However, the Flemish labour market is not homogeneous and it is possible to identify a number of sub-regional differences. The highest level of unemployment was registered in the province of Antwerp (6.2%), followed by Limburg and Flemish Brabant both at around 5%. With the exception of West Flanders, unemployment increased in all provinces between 2007 and 2013. In particular, Flemish Brabant showed a deep increase, with unemployment rate rising from 3.4% in 2007 to 5% in 2014. Educational attainments also vary across Flemish provinces. The province of Flemish Brabant has a significantly higher percentage of population with tertiary education than the other four provinces at 44.3% in 2013. Limburg shows the lowest rate at 28.7% in 2013. Between 2004 and 2013, the share of people with tertiary education increased but with different intensity. Limburg had a very low increase at 1.3 percentage points, while in West Flanders the rate grew by 8 percentage points.

As part of its Programme for the International Assessment of Adult Competencies (PIAAC), the OECD collects and analyses data that assist governments in assessing, monitoring and analysing the level and distribution of skills among their adult populations as well as the utilisation of skills in different contexts. It measures the key cognitive and workplace skills needed for individuals to participate in society and for economies to prosper.

PIAAC looks at skills in three domains namely literacy, numeracy and problem solving and for each of them, proficiency scores are derived on a scale ranging from 0 to 500 points. The results from the PIAAC survey show that adults in Flanders have above average proficiency in literacy and numeracy and average proficiency in problem solving in technology-rich environments compared with other countries who participated in the survey (OECD, 2013). Young adults in Flanders (16-24 years old) have above average proficiency in literacy, numeracy, and problem solving in technology rich environments compared with other OECD countries (OECD, 2013).

Proficiency in literacy, numeracy, and problem solving differs significant when looking at the results at the regional level in Flanders (see Figure 2.6). The adults in Flemish-Brabant show relatively higher levels of literacy, numeracy, and problem solving skills. Antwerp also has relatively high scores especially in numeracy and problem solving. The region of Limburg shows a relatively lower level of proficiency in literacy and problem solving skills when compared to other regions in Flanders. Numeracy was the lowest in East Flanders. Mobility may partly explain the strong regional variation with more proficient individuals likely to move to areas where there are higher skilled jobs (e.g. Antwerp and Brussels – of which Flemish Brabant is the periphery). Understanding these regional differences in skills is important as individuals with lower levels of literacy are more likely to have poorer labour market outcomes relative to those with higher skills.

Figure 2.6. **OECD Survey of Adult Skills, results across regions in Flanders**

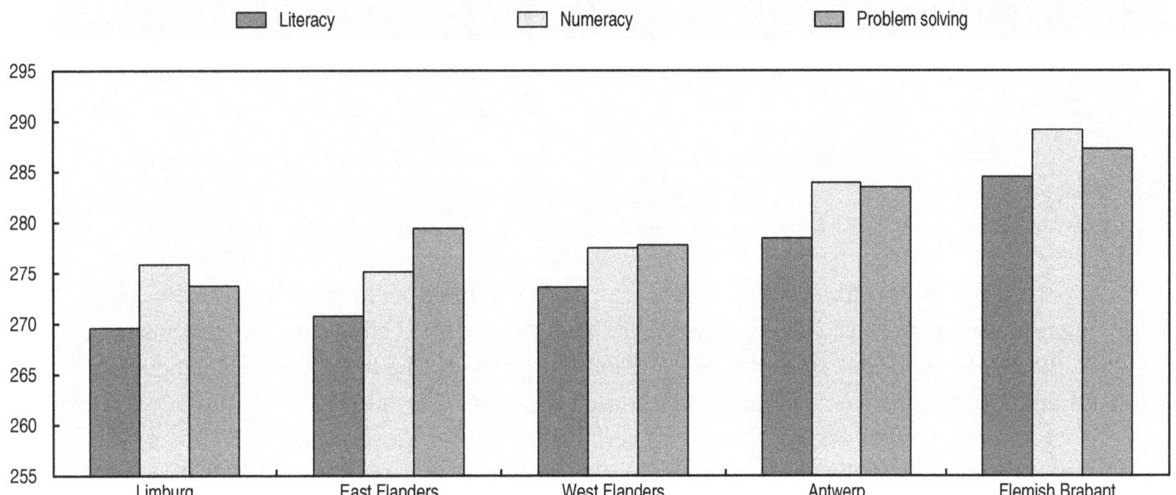

Source: *OECD Skills Outlook 2013: First Results from the Survey of Adult Skills*, OECD Publishing, Paris, *http://dx.doi.org/10.1787/9789264204256-en*.

The environmental and resource productivity of the economy

This group of indicators captures "the efficiency with which economic activities – both production and consumption – use energy, other natural resources (such as water) and environmental services from natural capital" (OECD, 2014a). This criteria is rarely quantified in economic models and accounting frameworks. For Flanders and benchmarking regions and countries, only two indicators were available: CO_2 emissions per capita and the volume of municipal waste. It is worth highlighting that they are from 2008 and more recent updates were not available. However they do provide an indication of how Flanders compares to its benchmarks.

Carbon and energy productivity

CO_2 emissions represent the major source of greenhouse gas (GHG) emissions and have a significant impact on climate change and the global temperature increase. Climate change can have a number of significant short and long-term effects that can impact human well-being, economic and environmental activities. In relation to CO_2 emissions per capita, three measures were available: total emissions, emissions from the transport sector and emissions from the energy sector (see Figure 2.7 below). Both at the European and global level, these two sectors together represent the vast majority of the CO_2 emissions (European Commission, 2014; IEA, 2013).

Figure 2.7. **CO_2 emissions per capita, European regions, 2008**

Tonnes per inhabitant

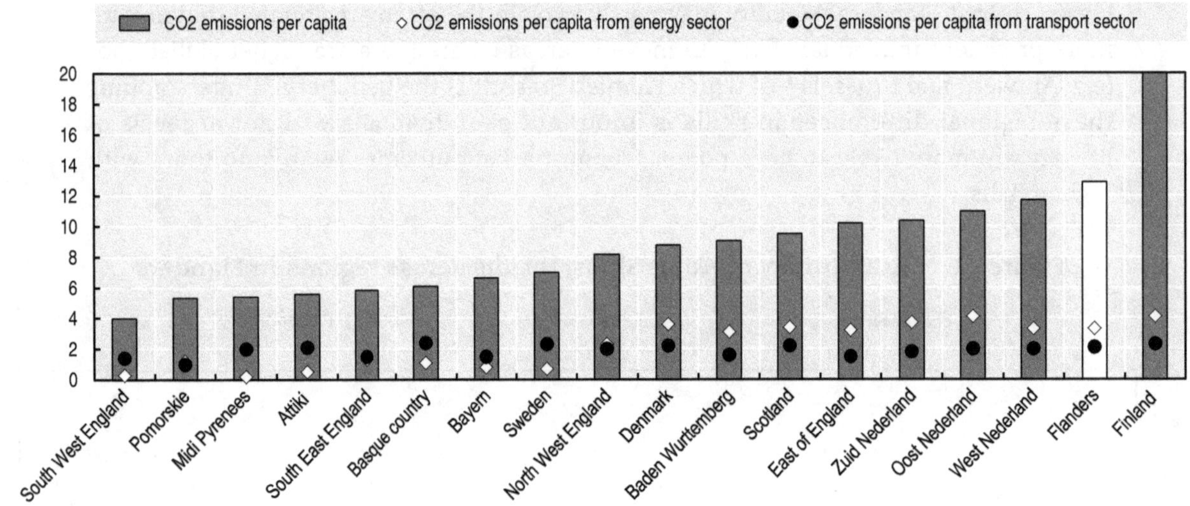

Source: OECD (2016), "Large regions, TL2: Social indicators", *OECD Regional Statistics* (database), *http://dx.doi.org/10.1787/data-00524-en.*

In Flanders CO_2 emissions per capita, expressed in tonnes per inhabitant, were the second highest among the selected benchmarks, just after Finland and before the three regions in the Netherlands. Emissions from the energy sector are close to the average of the benchmarks whereas emissions from transport are relatively higher. The latter is probably due to the geography of Flanders and its dense transport infrastructures (Government of Flanders, 2013). In the framework of the Flanders Mobility Plan, actions (such as investing in technological innovation to streamline public transport, the introduction of the Kilometer Charge for trucks and supporting multi-model transport) have already been taken to reduce emissions from road transport, which is the main source of CO_2 transport related emissions in the region.

Resource productivity: materials, nutrients, water

The second indicator available for Flanders is the volume of municipal waste per capita. This is calculated by dividing a daily average of waste generated in household and business by the total population. Waste contributes to the production of GHG and in particular to methane that is released during the breakdown of organic matter in landfills. Recycling and waste reduction can contribute in the long term to the reduction of GHG emissions and saving energy (UNEP, 2010). Data shows that around 20% of raw materials extracted worldwide end up as waste, and OECD countries contribute to the production of around one third of global waste (OECD, 2015).

For this indicator Flanders performs relatively well, just after Attica (Greece) and Pomorskie (Poland). However this data should be interpreted carefully as the definition only provides a partial picture of environmental issues related to waste. It should be complemented with information on waste management practices and costs and information on consumption levels and patterns.

In Flanders waste initiatives are managed by the Public Waste Agency of Flanders (OVAM) and waste prevention through sustainable resource management is seen as the main area of intervention. In addition to reducing waste, initiatives promote re-use, recycling, and incineration instead of landfill, which is the most polluting method of disposing waste. The efficiency of waste management is a result of a good co-ordination between regional policies and local initiatives.

Figure 2.8. **Volume of municipal waste, European regions, 2008**

Kilograms per capita, hundreds

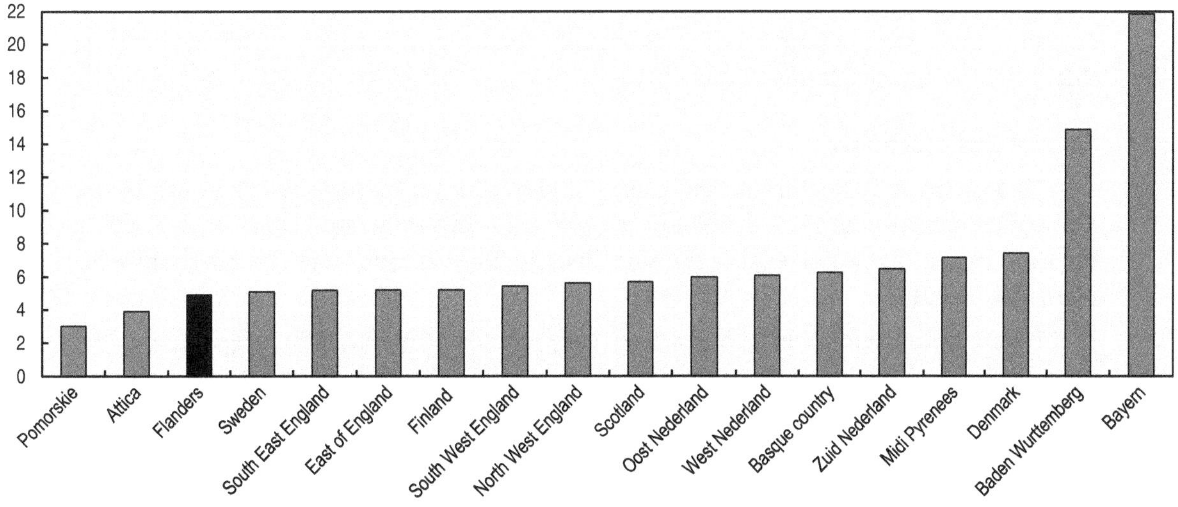

Source: OECD (2016), "OECD Regional Statistics: Large regions, TL2 – Social indicators (Edition 2015)", *OECD Regional Statistics* (database), *http://dx.doi.org/10.1787/003617aa-en.*

Analysis at the local level

In relation to this group of indicators, only data on CO_2 emissions was available at the local level. As shown in Table 2.2, the province with the highest share of CO_2 emissions per capita, measured in tonnes per inhabitants, is Flemish Brabant (15.4) while the province of West Flanders shows the lowest levels of emissions (7.75).

When looking at the emissions by sector, the situation is very different. For Limburg and East Flanders more than 40% of the emissions are produced from the energy sector and only 16% in Flemish Brabant. The emissions from the transport sector are similar across all provinces except West Flanders that shows a particularly high share (27%).

Table 2.2. **CO_2 emissions in Flemish provinces, 2008**

	Province Antwerpen	Province Limburg	Province Oost-Vlaanderen	Province Vlaams-Brabant	Province West-Vlaanderen
CO_2 emissions per capita (tonnes per inhabitant)	13.7	13.9	13.5	15.4	7.7
Share of CO_2 emissions from the energy sector (%)	20.5	42.2	42.3	15.9	3.1
Share of CO_2 emissions from the transport sector (%)	13.7	14.8	15.1	15.8	27

Source: OECD (2016), "Large regions, TL2: Social indicators", *OECD Regional Statistics* (database), *http://dx.doi.org/10.1787/data-00524-en.*

Multi-factor productivity

Multi-factor productivity (MFP) is a key determinant of long-term growth of output, income and living standards. It is measured using the standard production function, whereby output is derived using labour and capital input factors.

In the framework of the Green Growth strategy, the OECD has started working on the identification of environmentally-adjusted multi-factor productivity (MFP) in order to measure a country's ability to generate income from a given set of inputs (typically, labour and produced capital) while also accounting for the consumption of natural resources and production of undesirable environmental outputs. This exercise consists of adjusting the measurement framework to include both environmental inputs (natural resources) and environmental outputs (undesirable outputs like emissions). Because of the lack of data, this indicator is not included in this study.

The natural asset base

This group of indicators provides an indication of the natural resource stock, the availability of non-renewable stock and the biological diversity and ecosystems. Keeping the asset base intact would ensure the sustainability of economic growth and human well-being (OECD, 2014a).

The indicators within this group are not easy to find at the sub-national level and when they exist, comparability across countries is not possible. In order to give an idea on how Flanders performs, data for Belgium has been used instead and comparisons have been made with neighbouring countries (France, Germany and the Netherlands) and selected countries from the benchmarks (Denmark, Finland and Sweden). When making comparisons, it should be kept in mind that intra-national differences can be significant and assumptions on performance should be made only if national data is complemented with regional data.

Renewable stocks water, forest, fish resources

Water availability significantly affects people, life and sustainability. Water is used in many different ways, including irrigation of crops, cooling in power plants, refineries and steel industries and in food production. Figure 2.9 shows the renewable freshwater resources per capita for Belgium and the other benchmarking regions and countries. This measure is used both by the OECD and European Environment Agency to quantify the availability of fresh water and allow international comparisons. With a value of 1 800 cubic meters per capita, Belgium is towards the bottom of the distribution close to Poland and Germany. On the contrary, Sweden and Finland have very high renewable water resources both around 20 000 cubic meters per capita.

Nevertheless Belgium, and more precisely Flanders, is the largest European producer of frozen vegetables (25% of Europe's supply of frozen vegetables is produced in Flanders). In addition, the port of Antwerp represents one of the largest chemical clusters worldwide.

Another relevant indicator relates to water abstraction, expressed as a percentage of total renewable resources (see Figure 2.12 below). This indicator, also known as water stress, gives an idea of the level of sustainability of water resource management. It should be noted that the national indicator may hide significant territorial differences and should be complemented with information at sub-national level (OECD, 2014).

Figure 2.9. **Renewable freshwater resources per capita, latest year available**
1 000 m^3/capita

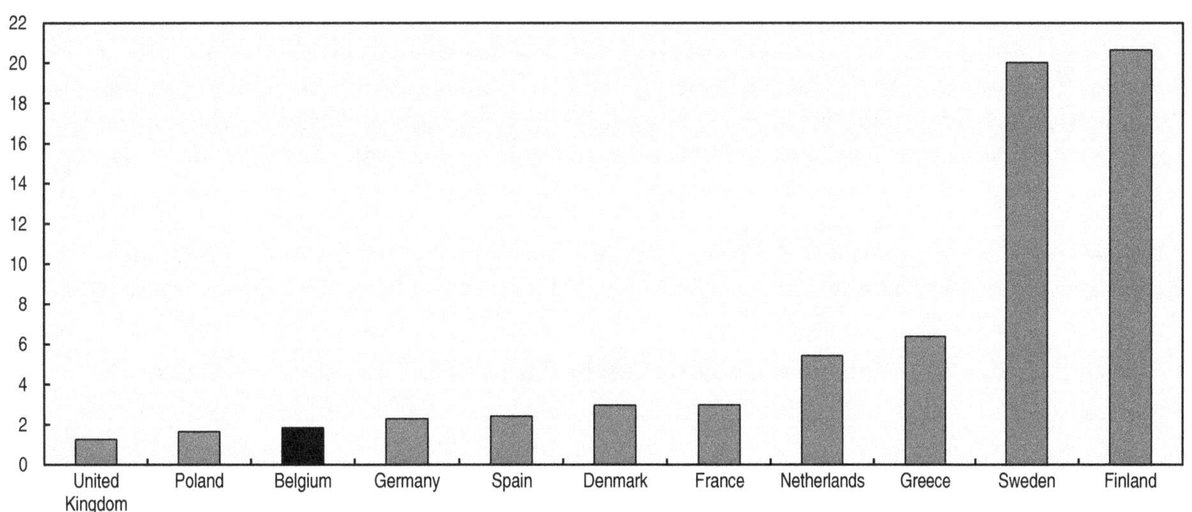

Source: OECD (2011), *Towards Green Growth: Monitoring Progress: OECD Indicators*, OECD Publishing, Paris, *http://dx.doi.org/10.1787/9789264111356-en*.

Among the benchmarking countries and regions, Belgium has the highest share of water abstraction from total available resources, closely followed by Spain. With a value of 30%, it shows a medium level of water stress. Nordic countries, namely Denmark, Finland and Sweden show very low values and have no water stress.

Forests are an important source of growth in terms of production, and reservoirs for biodiversity. Therefore it is fundamental to limit the effects of human activities and implement good management practices for forest resources. Data shows that among the countries in this study, Finland and Sweden have the highest share of forests, which compose 73% and 69% respectively of the total land area. Belgium's land mass is composed of 22% forests. Trend data do not show significant changes over the last 10 years.

Analysis at the local level

The Vlakwa study presented in Box 2.1 also shows data by province. When comparing them, it is interesting to note that East Flanders abstracts nearly two thirds of the water of the region, followed by Antwerp (28%). The other provinces all show values below 5%. The share of abstraction doesn't seem to have a direct link with the number of firms in the province – for example, West Flanders abstracts only 2% of water resources but has more than 30% of the firms of the region.

Box 2.1. **The socio-economic importance of water in Flanders**

The Flemish Knowledge Centre Water (VLAKWA) has recently conducted a study aimed to identify water sensitive industries and will help to develop specific actions and policies to ensure their competitiveness. The analysis shows that the sector which abstracts the most water is the energy sector, followed by the chemical industry and the industry operating in the manufacturing of cokes and refined petroleum products. In these sectors, most of the abstracted water is used as cooling water. When looking at sectors that use water for consumption and not for cooling, the chemical industry is the one that uses the most water, followed by drinking water companies, agriculture, food manufacturing and metal industry.

Box 2.1. **The socio-economic importance of water in Flanders** *(cont.)*

The study also looked at the impact of an increase in water costs on future productivity, as measured by gross value added by sector. Sectors that seem most sensitive towards an increase in water costs are manufacturing of chemical products, drinking water companies, agricultural sector, food processing companies, manufacturing of basic metals and energy production. Based on the consumption, employment and impact of price water increase, the study identified "water-intensive" industrial sectors that are particularly at risk in the long-term. Water intensive industries have a strong impact on employment in Flanders. On average, 1 out of 6 employees (16.7%) works in one of the 15 sectors (total of 100 sectors) with the highest water uptake. Differences exist across provinces with West Flanders having the highest share of employment in these sectors (18.2%) and Flemish Brabant having the lowest (13%).

Figure 2.10. **Total water abstraction (millions of m³) by sector, year 2010**

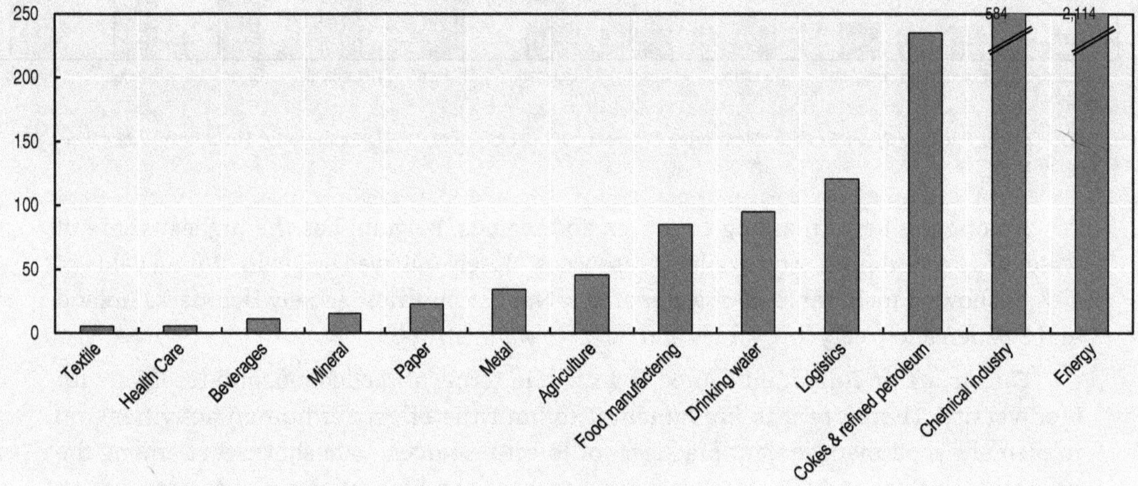

Source: Tax database Flanders Environment Agency (VMM).

Figure 2.11. **Share of employment in the 15 most water intensive industries by province, 2010**

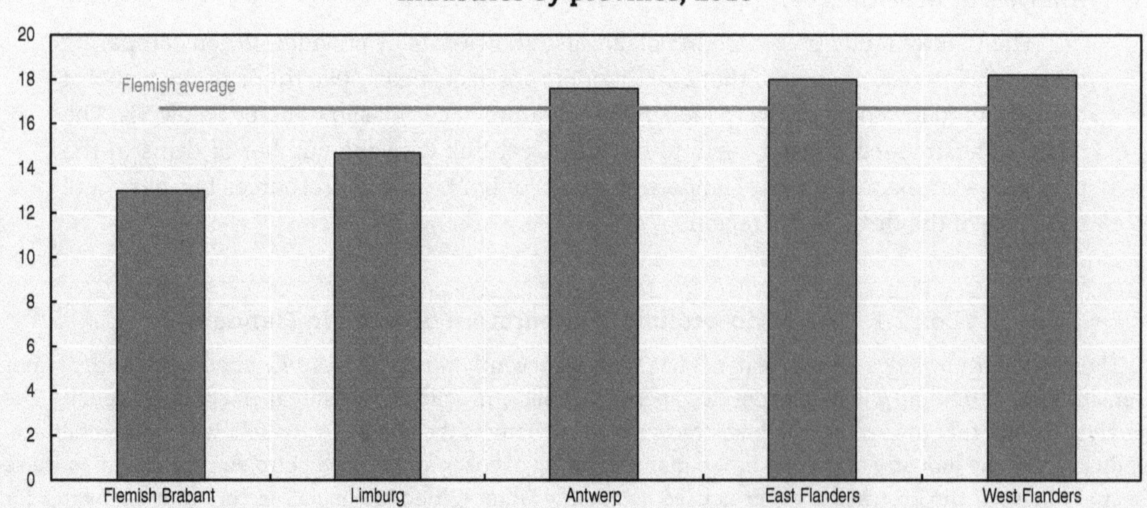

Source: VLAKWA (2013) – Vlaams Kenniscentrum Water "Socioeconomic importance of water in Flanders".

Figure 2.12. **Water abstraction, latest year available**

As a % of renewable resource

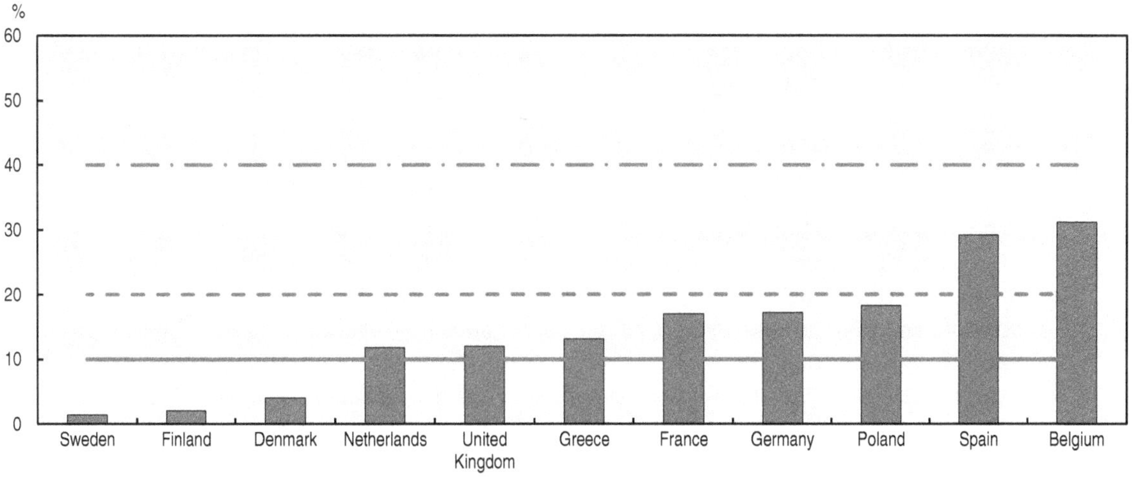

Note: Water stress below 10% = no stress; 10-20% = low stress; 20-40% = medium stress; above 40% = severe stress.

Source: OECD (2012), *Water stress*, OECD countries: 2009 or latest year available; water abstractions as a % of renewable resource, in *OECD Environmental Outlook*, OECD Publishing, Paris, *http://dx.doi.org/10.1787/env_outlook-2012-graph69-en.*

Average annual water consumption per firm (excluding cooling water) also varies by province, with West Flanders and Flemish-Brabant showing values that are around a fifth lower than those in Antwerp. This is probably influenced by the industrial sectors present in each province.

Non-renewable stocks: mineral resources

This indicator covers the available stocks of reserves of non-renewable stocks like minerals and relative extraction rates. It is not included in this study because of a lack of data.

Biodiversity and ecosystems

A number of studies conducted by international organisations, including the Institute for European Environmental Policy, UNCTAD, UNEP and the OECD, highlight that biodiversity, defined as the diversity of living organisms, is strictly linked to the sustainability of the economy. It relates to both human wellbeing through the provision of water, fisheries, timber, etc. and economic growth through the development of markets for ecosystem services and goods. However, conservation of biodiversity is one of the main concerns for a number of OECD countries (OECD, 2012).

In 2007, the European Commission and Germany launched the TEEB study (The Economics of Ecosystems and Biodiversity) with the objective of raising awareness of the value of biodiversity and ecosystem services and to facilitate the development of cost-effective policy responses.

Data on this theme only exist for biodiversity related to threatened species, including mammals, birds and vascular plants. The "threatened" category refers to species "critically endangered", "endangered" or "vulnerable" in relation to their risk of extinction. On these three indicators, Belgium shows values that range between 21% and 23% of the number of known or assessed species. The Netherlands show similar figures, while Germany show the highest figures and Finland the lowest. Data on trends of these indicators are not available for the countries studied in this report.

The environmental dimension of quality of life

This group of indicators assesses the direct impacts of the environment on people's lives, through for example access to safe, sufficient water of adequate quality or the damaging effects of air pollution, as well as environmental services and amenities offered to the population (see Box 2.2 and Box 2.3).

Box 2.2. **The importance of water in improving quality of life**

In the framework of the OECD Green Growth strategy, only data on air pollution are taken into consideration when measuring the environmental dimension of quality of life. This is probably due to the lack of comparable data on other dimensions. Water in particular represents an essential resource for people's lives and more broadly for the economy. A number of initiatives at the European level have been implemented to protect water resources. The EU Water Framework Directive (WFD) is designed to protect European waters, achieve good ecological status and enable sustainable use. The 2012 'Blueprint to safeguard Europe's water resources' was implemented with the objective of ensuring that a sufficient quantity of good quality water is available for people's needs, the economy and the environment throughout the EU.

Despite the growing interest in this field, data on water quality are not always comparable across countries. For example, data collected from the joint questionnaire on inland waters realised by Eurostat and the OECD was completed on a voluntary basis. The datasets are therefore incomplete, which limits their usability. Interestingly, data is also collected at the regional level to develop a smaller data set on NUTS2 regions and River Basin Districts (regions defined in terms of hydrology). This indicates good potential for the future use of local level data.

Box 2.3. **Water Management Policies at the OECD**

In recognition of the importance of water to quality of life, the OECD has investigated the nexus between water management and future green growth.

The publication 'Water and Innovation for Green Growth' (2015) notes that effective and efficient water management can catalyse green growth. In addition, the OECD promotes a risk management approach to addressing water security risks and stresses the infrastructure investment required to ensure a sustainable water supply to underpin economic growth in the future. Technical and non-technical innovation can reduce the costs associated with effective water management.

Examples of water-related innovation can be found in the publication "Water and Cities: Ensuring Sustainable Futures" publication. The study notes a variety of opportunities for disruptive technical innovation, including smart water cities, decentralised technologies and distributed water management systems for efficient use of water in urban contexts. Examples of innovative water use in Hamburg, Germany, Fukuoka City. Japan, Suwon, Korea and San Francisco, California have found that the incorporation of new information and communications technology innovations have improved sustainable water usage. Other aspects of non-technical innovation can include the use of non-potable water, water sensitive urban design and sustainable drainage.

Successful water management is ultimately reliant on increasing engagement with key stakeholder groups and integrating policy responses. The unique scale of water resource

Box 2.3. **Water Management Policies at the OECD** *(cont.)*

management necessitates the creation of synergies within and between different layers of government, the private sector, service providers, regulators, non-governmental organisations and citizen groups. The OECD's recent work on 'Integrated can promotes the sustainable use of water resources. The OECD investigated this topic further through its recent work on "Stakeholder Engagement for Inclusive Water Governance". This publication builds upon other OECD work on water governance, including the 2007 OECD Horizontal Project on "Sustainable Financing to Ensure Affordable Access to Water and Sanitation".

Source: OECD Water and Innovation for Green Growth: Policy Perspectives 2015, OECD Stakeholder Engagement for Inclusive Water Governance 2015, OECD Water and Cities: Ensuring Sustainable Futures 2015.

The quality of the environment can have an impact on human well-being. More specifically a degraded environment can affect health, labour productivity and more broadly lower the quality of life. Indicators in this group monitor the human exposure to air pollution and the public access to environmental services (services which provide for physiological as well as recreational and related needs of human beings). Data at the regional level is only available on the air quality dimension for a specific pollution indicator – PM 2.5 (PM 2.5 measured in micrograms per cubic metres).

Environmental health and risks

In order to measure the level of human exposure to air pollution, a comparable indicator is the level of fine particulates (PM 2.5 measured in micrograms per cubic metres) derived from satellite-based measurements. This is also used as the only environment measure for the OECD Regional Well-being initiative.

The figure below shows how Flanders compares to the benchmarks. In 2000, the region had the highest levels of PM 2.5 at 18.6 micrograms per cubic metres, followed by West Netherlands and Bavaria. Sweden and Finland have the lowest levels of PM 2.5.

A small decrease has been registered in Flanders between 2000 and 2013 but it still remains among the countries and regions with the highest levels of particulates. Bavaria has showed a significant change over time moving from 18.3 micrograms in 2000 to 14.7 in 2013.

The transportation sector and in particular cars contribute to the emission of air pollutants. Looking at private vehicle ownership could be a useful proxy to add information on air pollution. Data availability was limited for this indicator and comparability across countries and regions is possible only between 2007 and 2010. However, even if the timeframe is quite short, it is possible to identify interesting patterns.

In 2010 Flanders was in the middle of the distribution with 500 cars per 1 000 inhabitants. This result is comparable to eastern and southern Netherlands and east England. The number of cars is particularly low in Denmark (375 cars per 1 000 inhabitants) and relatively high in the south-east England (543 cars per 1 000 inhabitants) and in Bavaria (548 cars per 1 000 inhabitants).

In Flanders the number of cars has increased by around 2% which is negligible in comparison to other benchmarks (for example in Pomorskie, growth was 17%). Nevertheless the German regions showed a very significant decrease of cars (around 10% in both regions) which might be a sign that efforts have been made to shift to alternative modes of transport.

Figure 2.13. **Air pollution, level of PM2.5, 2000 and 2013**

Micrograms per cubic metres

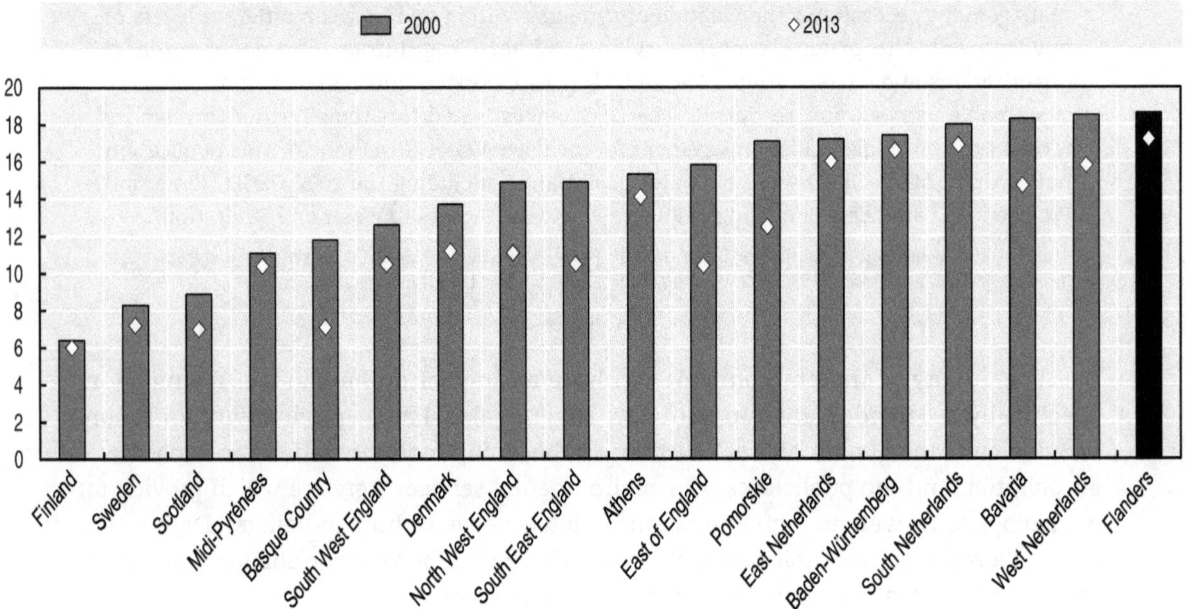

Source: OECD (2016), "Regional well-being", *OECD Regional Statistics* (database), *http://dx.doi.org/10.1787/data-00707-en.*

Analysis at the local level

A recent report produced by three government agencies: the Inter-regional Environment Office, the Flemish Institute for Technological Research and the Flemish Environment Agency confirm the very high levels of particulates in Flanders and shows interesting patterns across localities in the region. Pollution is particularly concentrated around Antwerp and Ghent but the level is high across the entire region.

Environmental services and amenities

Indicators in this group include the level of public access to environmental services and amenities. A relevant indicator that relates to water is wastewater treatment levels which is measured by the OECD at the national level. This dataset provides information on the level of public equipment installed by countries to manage and reduce water pollution.

Figure 2.14 below shows sewage treatment connection rates, i.e. the percentage of the population connected to a wastewater treatment plant. "Connected" means actually connected to a wastewater treatment plant through a public sewage network. It does not take into account independent private facilities. The figure shows that Belgium has a relatively low level of connection compared to the other benchmarking countries.

Economic opportunities and policy responses

This group of indicators measures the level of technology and innovation, international financial flows and the effectiveness of policy in delivering green growth.

Both governments and businesses have an important role in reducing the effects of climate change and promoting green growth. This group of indicators covers a broad range of topics that will be analysed in more detail in the following paragraphs.

Figure 2.14. **Sewage treatment connection rates, % of population, 2012 or most recent year**

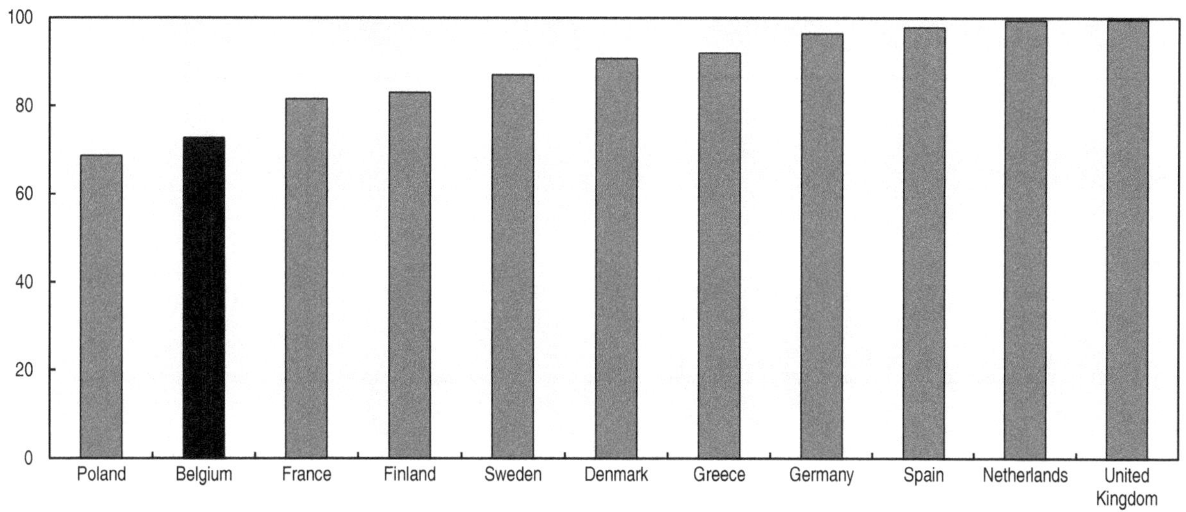

Note: Data for Belgium refers to 2009 and for Germany and the United Kingdom to 2010.
Source: OECD (2015), Sewage treatment connection rates, % of population, in *Environment at a Glance 2015*, OECD Publishing, Paris, *http://dx.doi.org/10.1787/9789264235199-table30-en*.

Technology and innovation

Technology and innovation are important drivers for productivity and job creation. They can also contribute to better management of energy, water, materials and land use and can consequently improve productivity and resource efficiency. Governments can also contribute by promoting education in fields related to green technologies, investing in research and development and supporting new forms of eco-innovation. Governments can promote the growth of greener economic activities to support resource efficiency and recovery instead of traditional carbon- and resource-intensive industries (OECD, 2014b). This has become a more urgent policy priority due to societal and global challenges, such as climate change, resource scarcity, ageing of population, globalisation and urbanisation.

According to the OECD, R&D is defined as "creative work undertaken on a systematic basis in order to increase the stock of knowledge, including knowledge of man, culture and society, and the use of this stock of knowledge to devise new applications" (OECD, 2002a). R&D expenditure as a percentage of GDP is one of the most common indicators used to measure the intensity of an economy in generating new knowledge. In OECD countries, R&D expenditure performed by the business sector represents the highest share of total R&D expenditures as a percentage of GDP. Data on R&D expenditure for benchmark regions and countries is available until 2011. More recent data (2013) is available but at the national level only. This is shown in Figure 2.16.

Figure 2.15 below shows that significant differences exist across countries. Midi Pyrénées and Baden-Württemberg are the regions that invest the most in R&D (both at 5.1% of GDP), while Athens and Pomorskie are those who invest the least (0.8% and 0.7% respectively). Flanders is in the middle of the distribution with expenditure in R&D at 2.4%. All countries and regions except the East of England, Sweden and the South Netherlands have increased total R&D expenditure between 2003 and 2011.

In order to also explore the relationship between innovation and green growth, it is useful to look at the share of government R&D budgets for energy and the environment. This indicator exists only at the national level and shows the public investment in basic and

Figure 2.15. **Total R&D expenditure as percentage of GDP, 2003 and 2011**

Source: OECD (2016), "Regional innovation", *OECD Regional Statistics* (database), *http://dx.doi.org/10.1787/1c89e05a-en.*

long-term research. As shown in Figure 2.16 below, the share of government budget appropriations or outlays for R&D (GBAORD) invested in research on energy and the environment varies significantly across countries both in terms of quantity and composition. Belgium invests 4.5% of its GDP for energy and environment (2.2% and 2.3%). This is higher than in the United Kingdom and the Netherlands. Countries with the highest share of investment in these sectors are Finland, France and Germany. Interestingly, R&D investment in energy is greater than R&D investment in environment in all of these countries.

Figure 2.16. **Government R&D budgets for energy and the environment, 2013 or latest year**

As a percentage of total government R&D budget

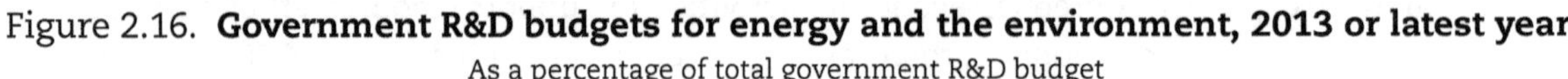

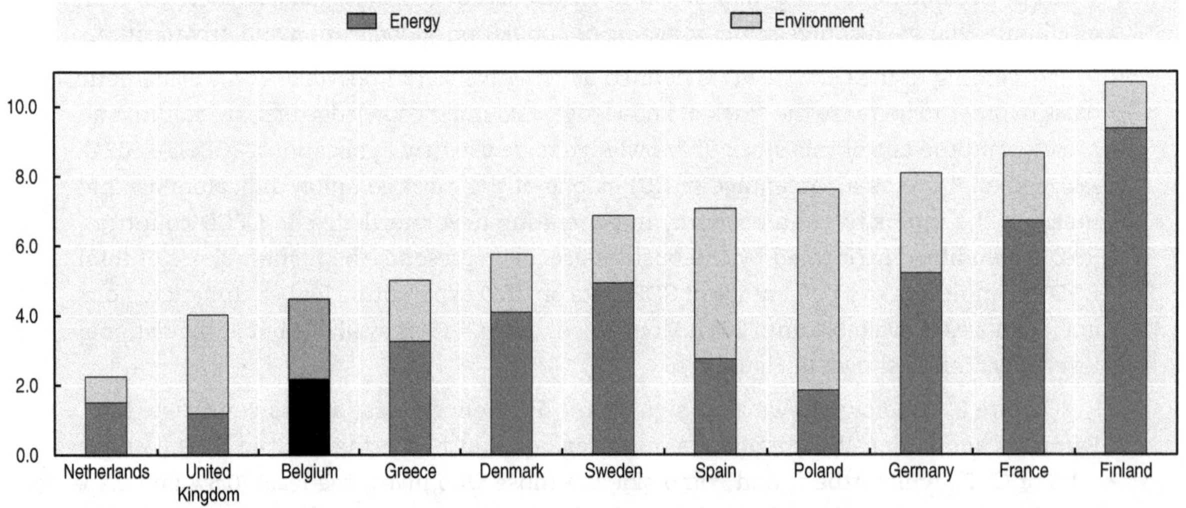

Source: OECD (2014), *OECD Science, Technology and Industry Outlook 2014*, OECD Publishing, Paris, *http://dx.doi.org/10.1787/sti_outlook-2014-en.*

Patent applications data measures the output of research and technology through the count of inventions per country. An application for a patent has to meet certain requirements: the invention must be novel, involve a (non-obvious) inventive step and be capable of industrial application (OECD, 2001).

Measuring patent applications is not an easy task because definitions and data collection methods vary significantly across countries. In order to overcome these problems, the OECD has created a patent database which allows international comparisons and provides a good level of disaggregation in terms of field. This enables analysis of innovation in green and environmental related technologies.

Patent applications in green technologies are particularly high in the German regions (with 248 and 241 patents in this sector). They are followed by Denmark, Sweden and South Netherlands that have around 100 patent applications. Similarly to R&D expenditure, Flanders is in the middle of the distribution, with 28 patent applications.

Figure 2.17. **Patent applications in green technologies, 2007**

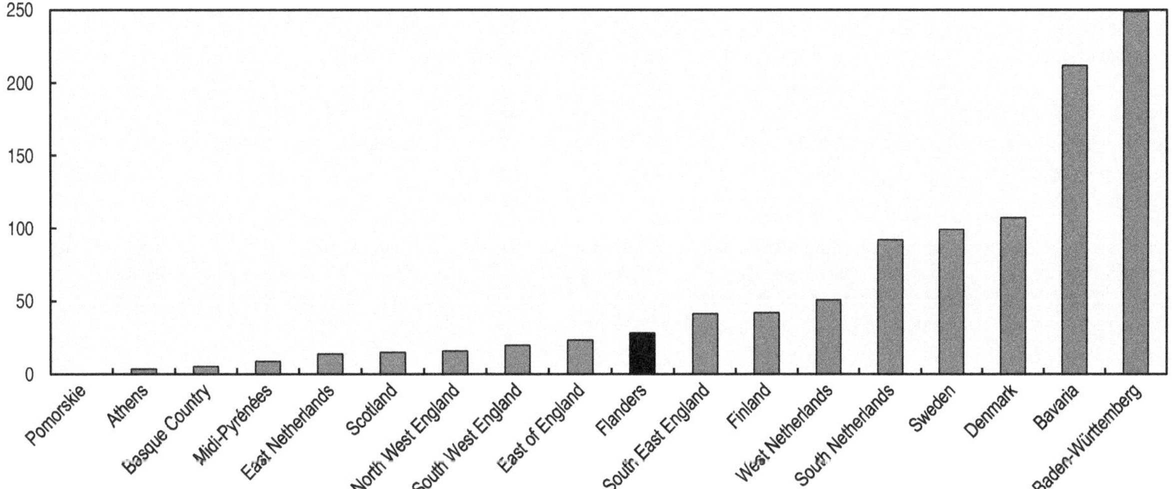

Source: OECD (2016), "Regional innovation", *OECD Regional Statistics* (database), *http://dx.doi.org/10.1787/1c89e05a-en.*

More detailed information on patents in environment-related technologies can be found in Table 2.3. As the number of patents varies significantly across countries, the most interesting aspect of the table is to determine which countries and regions have the highest number of patents. Most regions (Flanders, Denmark, Athens, East and West Netherlands, South East and South West of England) apply for patents related to energy generation from renewable and non-fossil sources. The second technological field is air emissions abatement and fuel efficiency in transport. This represents the main area of patent applications in Midi-Pyrénées, Baden-Württemberg, Bavaria, Sweden and the East of England. Finland and the North West of England excelled at patenting innovations in general environmental management (air, water and waste), whereas the South Netherland patents innovations in energy efficiency in buildings and lighting.

Environmental goods and services

The production of environmental goods and services (EGS) can contribute to the creation of employment and green growth. Production of EGS is still limited as it is influenced by regulation, policy objectives and instruments to make the sector more competitive. Developing the right skills, investing in targeted training and strengthening the knowledge sharing across firms can be useful tools to increase employment and value added in the EGS sector (OECD, 2014a; OECD, 2014b).

Table 2.3. **Patents in environment-related technologies, 2009**

	Technologies specific to climate change mitigation	Emissions abatement and fuel efficiency in transportation	Technologies with potential or indirect contribution to emissions mitigation	Energy generation from renewable and non-fossil sources	Energy efficiency in buildings and lighting	General Environmental Management (air, water, waste)	Combustion technologies with mitigation potential (eg using fossil fuels, biomass, waste etc.)
Flemish Region	1	2.8	7.6	**14.4**	7.2	13.4	..
Denmark	3.1	13	8.5	**126.9**	11.5	21.2	3.3
Finland	1	14.3	9.7	34.3	7	**42.8**	4
Midi-Pyrénées	0.3	**10.2**	6.2	8.4	1.5	8.6	..
Baden-Württemberg	5.5	**414.5**	137.4	123.5	16.9	103.6	2
Bavaria	12.8	**171.8**	68.1	131.7	42.2	87.3	22.4
Athens	..	1	0.3	**6.1**	2.3	1	..
East Netherlands	0.7	..	5	**16.9**	1.5	11.7	..
West Netherlands	19.9	4.5	4	**56.3**	2.3	22.8	1
South Netherlands	1	8	7.5	15	**76**	15.2	0.2
Sweden	5.5	**124.6**	19.9	56.7	12.1	71.8	5
North West England	1.5	3.3	7.9	11.6	3	**14.6**	..
East of England	0.5	**21.4**	7.7	8.3	8.7	17.8	0.2
South East England	3	21.8	18.9	**34.4**	8	17.5	3.1
South West England	0.7	0.9	3	**15.7**	1.5	10.2	2.3

Note: Data for Pomorskie and Basque Country were excluded from the analysis because data was missing for many categories of patents. More information on the definition of the categories in the table can be found here: *www.oecd.org/env/consumption-innovation/indicator.htm.*
Source: OECD (2015), "Patents in environment-related technologies: Technology diffusion and patent protection (Edition 2015)", *OECD Environment Statistics* (database), *http://dx.doi.org/10.1787/b06b7863-en.*

Data on these indicators do not exist at the regional level and the comparison will be done at the national level. According to the OECD definition, employment in sectors producing environmental goods and services is computed for selected countries and selected sectors and is expressed as a percentage of the total employment. The sectors covered include: rubber and plastics products (ISIC 22, rev.4) and water supply; sewerage, waste management and remediation activities (ISIC 36-39, rev.4).

Figure 2.18 shows trends in employment in selected environmental services for Belgium, neighbouring countries (France, Germany and the Netherlands) and selected countries from the benchmarks (Denmark, Finland and Sweden). Countries do not show very significant differences in terms of the share of employment in EGS sector, with Germany having 0.57% of total employment and the Netherlands 0.44%. Trends over time show an increase in Belgium, Sweden, France and Finland, stagnation in Denmark and the Netherlands and a decrease in Germany.

International financial flows

Public and private resources can enable the sharing of technology and good practices across countries. Measuring financial flows through official development assistance (ODA) to environment and renewable energy and targeting the objectives of the Rio Conventions (including, for example, biodiversity and climate change) is a useful measure to assess progress towards green growth. The relevance of this indicator is limited in relation to the scope of this study and therefore is not included.

Prices and transfers

Prices, taxes and regulations can influence production and consumption patterns. Environmental related taxes are instruments for the government to determine relative

Figure 2.18. **Trends in employment in sectors producing environmental goods and services**

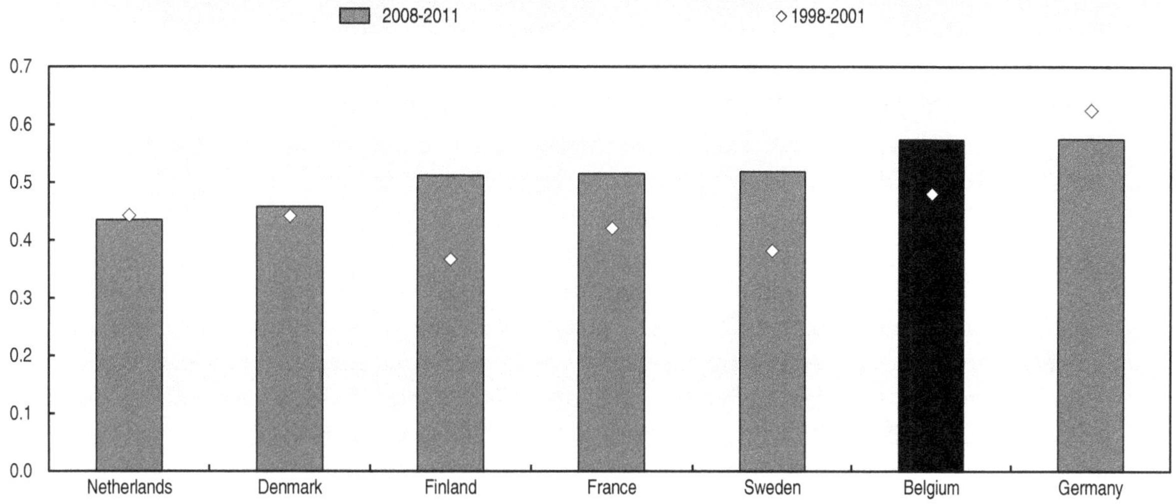

Source: OECD (2014), *Green Growth Indicators 2014*, OECD Publishing, Paris, *http://dx.doi.org/10.1787/9789264202030-en.*

prices for example of energy. This category follows the OECD definition and includes the following categories: i) energy products for transport purposes (petrol and diesel) and for stationary purposes (fossil fuels and electricity); ii) motor vehicles and transport (one-off import or sales taxes, recurrent taxes on registration or road use and other transport taxes); iii) waste management (final disposal, packaging and other waste-related product taxes); iv) ozone-depleting substances; and v) other taxes.

Environmental related taxes are still limited in many OECD countries and contribute to 2% of GDP. These data are generally presented together with labour taxation as these two measures have a direct impact on both employment and environment. A recent report shows that in order to boost economic growth, European countries should shift the tax burden from labour to energy, water, resources and environmental taxes as this would encourage employers to hire new people, boosting economic growth (European

Figure 2.19. **Total environmentally related taxes and labour tax revenue as % of GDP, 2012**

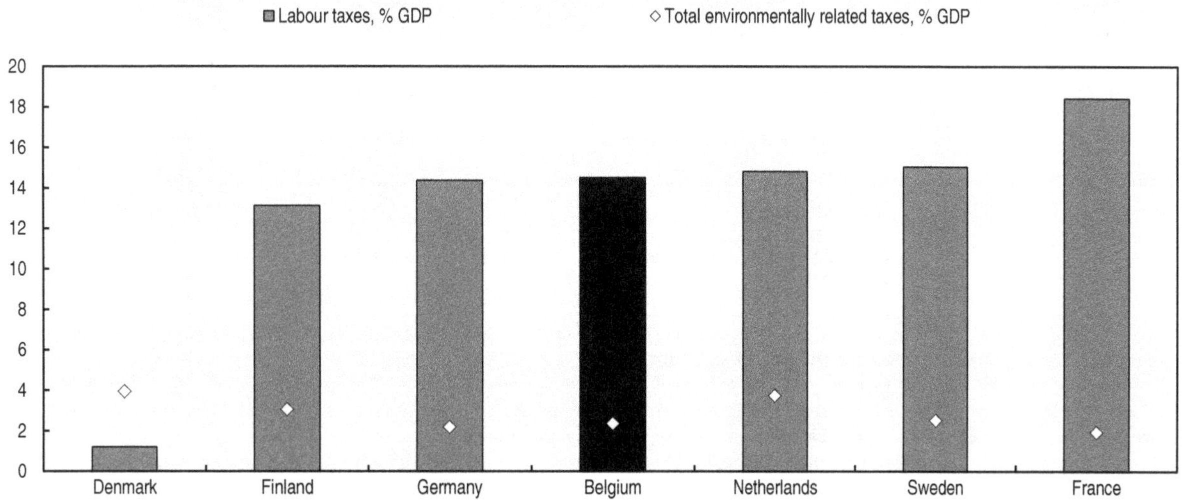

Source: OECD (2014), *Green Growth Indicators 2014*, OECD Publishing, Paris, *http://dx.doi.org/10.1787/9789264202030-en.*

Environment Agency, 2014). In the countries analysed in this study, environmental taxes range between 1.9% in France to 3.9% in Denmark. These two countries are also opposite in terms of labour taxation, with France having the highest share of GDP.

Skills and training and regulations and management approaches

The list of indicators under these two themes hasn't been developed yet by the OECD because of the limited data availability and comparability across countries.

Conclusions

The OECD Green Growth strategy has identified a number of indicators that help countries measure their progress towards a greener economy in a comprehensive way. This methodology has been used to compare Flanders to other selected benchmarking regions and countries in order to assess its relative level of "green". Table 2.4 below summarises the indicators analysed in this report. Nevertheless data availability remains a challenge and not all indicators could allow international comparisons at the regional level, for instance on water related issues. The Vlakwa study on the socio-economic importance of water in

Table 2.4. **Dashboard based on the OECD Green Growth framework**

Theme	Indicators	Level of analysis[1]	Evaluation in comparison to benchmark[2]
The socio-economic context and characteristics of growth	GDP per capita	Regional	□ ■ □
	Labour productivity	Regional	□ □ ■
	Unemployment rate	Regional	□ □ ■
	Youth unemployment rate	Regional	□ □ ■
The environmental and resource productivity of the economy	CO_2 emissions per capita	Regional	■ □ □
The natural asset base	Renewable freshwater resources per capita	National	■ □ □
	Water abstraction as % of renewable resources	National	■ □ □
	Biodiversity measured as share of threatened species	National	□ ■ □
The environmental dimension of quality of life	Air pollution, level of PM2.5	Regional	■ □ □
	Sewage treatment connection rates as % of population	National	■ □ □
Economic opportunities and policy responses	Total R&D expenditure as percentage of GDP	Regional	□ ■ □
	Government R&D budgets for energy and the environment	National	■ □ □
	Patent applications in green technologies	Regional	□ ■ □
	Trends in employment in sectors producing environmental goods and services	National	□ □ ■
	Total environmentally related taxes and labour tax revenue as % of GDP	National	□ ■ □

National analysis includes comparison with the following benchmark countries: Belgium, Denmark, Finland, France, Germany, Greece, Netherlands, Poland, Spain, Sweden and the United Kingdom.

1. *Regional analysis includes comparison with the following benchmark regions:* Flanders, Denmark, Finland, Midi Pyrenees, Baden Wurttemberg, Bayern, Attica/Athens, Oost Nederland, West Nederland, Zuid Nederland, Pomorskie, Basque country, Sweden, North West England, East of England, South East England, South West England, Scotland.
2. The shaded square refers to Flanders' place in the distribution amongst its regional and national peers for each indicator. Shading in the left-most square indicates that Flanders is amongst the lowest of the benchmarked regions or nations for the given indicator, while the opposite is true when the right-most square is shaded. Shading in the middle square indicates that Flanders scores around the median amongst benchmarked countries for the given indicator.

Flanders is a good example of how country/regional specific data can be collected. However if definitions are not internationally shared, comparability across countries will remain limited.

The transition to a green economy is linked to the socio-economic factors. With a well-educated population and a relative low unemployment rate in comparison to the other benchmarks, Flanders has favourable labour market conditions to facilitate the transition to a green economy. Flanders performs well compared to other benchmarks for some environment indicators – for instance, waste management. Nevertheless, Flanders is not performing as well for other indicators like air pollution and CO_2 emissions, especially from the transportation sector. In particular, Flanders is in the middle of the distribution in terms of innovation as measured through the investment in to R&D and patents applications and far behind the German regions of Bavaria and Baden Württemberg. This indicates that improvements in green innovation could be key to ensure Flanders' transition towards a greener economy.

References

European Commission (2014), *Climate change factsheet, http://ec.europa.eu/clima/publications/docs/factsheet_climate_change_2014_en.pdf.*

European Environment Agency (2014), *Resource-efficient green economy and EU policies.*

Government of Flanders (2013), *The Flemish Climate Policy Plan 2013-2020, www.lne.be/en/about/publications/flemish-climate-policy-plan-2013-2020-summary.pdf.*

Government of Flanders (2014), *Flanders outlook, a benchmarking of Flanders amongst the European regions.*

Government of Flanders (2010), *Mobility Plan for Flanders*, Mobility and Public Works Committee of the Flemish Government.

IEA (2013), *CO_2 emissions from fuel combustion Highlights*, International Energy Agency, *www.iea.org/publications/freepublications/publication/co2emissionsfromfuelcombustionhighlights2013.pdf.*

Martinez-Fernandez, C. et al. (2013), "Green Growth in the Benelux : Indicators of Local Transition to a Low-Carbon Economy in Cross-Border Regions", *OECD Local Economic and Employment Development (LEED) Working Papers*, No. 2013/09, Éditions OCDE, Paris, *http://dx.doi.org/10.1787/5k453xgh72ls-en.*

OECD (2015), *Material Resources, Productivity and the Environment*, OECD Green Growth Studies, OECD Publishing, Paris, *http://dx.doi.org/10.1787/9789264190504-en.*

OECD (2015b) *Water and Innovation for Green Growth: Policy Perspectives 2015*, OECD Publishing, Paris.

OECD (2015c), *Stakeholder Engagement for Inclusive Water Governance,* OECD Studies on Water, OECD Publishing, Paris, *http://dx.doi.org/10.1787/9789264231122-en.*

OECD (2015d), *Water and Cities: Ensuring Sustainable Futures*, OECD Studies on Water, OECD Publishing, Paris, *http://dx.doi.org/10.1787/9789264230149-en.*

OECD (2014a), *Green Growth Indicators 2014*, OECD Green Growth Studies, OECD Publishing, Paris, *http://dx.doi.org/10.1787/9789264202030-en.*

OECD (2014b), *Job Creation and Local Economic Development*, OECD Publishing, Paris, *http://dx.doi.org/10.1787/9789264215009-en.*

OECD (2013), *OECD Skills Outlook 2013: First Results from the Survey of Adult Skills*, OECD Publishing, Paris, *http://dx.doi.org/10.1787/9789264204256-en.*

OECD (2012), *OECD Environmental Outlook to 2050: The Consequences of Inaction*, OECD Publishing, Paris, *http://dx.doi.org/10.1787/9789264122246-en.*

OECD (2011), *Towards Green Growth*, OECD Green Growth Studies, OECD Publishing, Paris, *http://dx.doi.org/10.1787/9789264111318-en.*

OECD (2002a), *Frascati manual: Proposed standard practice for surveys on research and experimental development*, 6th edition.

OECD (2002b), *Integrating the Rio Conventions into Development Co-operation*, The DAC Guidelines, OECD Publishing, Paris, *http://dx.doi.org/10.1787/9789264176065-en*.

OECD (2001), *Using Patent Counts for Cross-Country Comparisons of Technology Output*.

UNEP (2010), *Waste and Climate Change: Global trends and strategy framework*.

VLAKWA (2013) *The socio-economic importance of water in Flanders* Vlaams KennisCentrum Water *www.vlakwa.be/fileadmin/media/pdf/20150605_samenvatting.pdf*.

Chapter 3

Policy framework and local initiatives for greening skills and jobs

This chapter explores the governance and implementation arrangements in place to promote sustainable skills and employment in Flanders, Belgium. It analyses policy developments with particular reference to the structure of the education system and the labour market, and investigates the role of public agencies in facilitating green initiatives at the local level.

The Flanders government has been working for a number of years to decouple economic growth from environmental impacts. Greening the economy is high on the agenda in a number of economic strategy documents. The Coalition Agreement of 2009 included an aim to establish a sustainable economy by 2020. This was translated into concrete and quantified objectives through two documents – Pact 2020 and Flanders in Action.

As part of the Flanders in Action strategy, Flanders has developed a new industrial policy (the New Industrial Policy – NIP), which found that the industry of the future will need to be both competitive and sustainable. A government policy note on this issue notes that industrial policy should not be about ad hoc intervention and "choosing" winners or "saving" losers, but rather creating smarter and better regulation, supported by the direction of state aid towards general long-term attainment targets such as a green economy. The aim is for "the industry of the future" to be greener, more social, more creative and more innovative, with products and services that are "made" in a different manner. The hope is to promote a faster restructuring of "lagging" sectors (those that are not innovating sufficiently), while supporting SME growth and internationalisation.

The Flanders in Action strategy also stressed the importance of competence development and work organisation so that skilled people are attracted towards working in industry and worker skills are maintained and upgraded. A public-private partnership created in 2009 named Flanders' Synergy is expected to play a role in helping industries evolve through workplace restructuring, workplace learning and innovation. Its objective is to help organisations create more attractive (workable) jobs and to become more agile, innovative and responsive to market needs. To this end, Flanders' Synergy conducts scientific research and helps disseminate practical examples and success stories through networking, training, and new business models and tools. The Flanders in Action strategy and the New Industrial policy are currently being replaced by new policy initiatives and instruments.

Box 3.1. **The evolution of Flanders industrial policy**

"Flanders in Action", the "New Industrial Policy" and the "smart specialisation" agenda

The **Flanders in Action** strategy developed in 2009 was based on a system approach for 13 transversal societal challenges. The overarching objective was to assist the implementation of "transitions" and systemic changes. Several of the 13 transversal themes were linked to the greening of the economy such as the new industrial policy, renewable energy and smart grid, sustainable living and building, sustainable materials management, smart mobility and towards a sustainable and creative city. Another transversal theme addresses the issue of skills for transition through the project "everyone participates, everyone is active" with the objective to create "excellence partnerships" for education and training.

The **New Industrial Policy** was one of the 13 transversal themes of Flanders in Action. It aimed to "create an innovative, green and socially strong industrial fabric by 2020" and

Box 3.1. **The evolution of Flanders industrial policy** *(cont.)*

stimulate the change in processes that is required for innovating existing and developing new industrial activity. To this end, in 2011, four policy pillars and fifty actions were identified to implement the New Industrial Policy:

- The "economic pillar", which addresses clusters of companies, knowledge institutions and education, and aims to boost the Factory of the Future.
- The "innovation pillar" focusses specifically on innovation that has an impact on transformation.
- The "social pillar" focuses on skills development and a new labour organisation.
- The "infrastructure pillar" enhances Flanders' appeal to the industry of the future.

Innovation policy and the link to the smart specialisation agenda

A new strategy for innovation policy is currently being developed. In September 2014, the government announced that the "label" of Flanders in Action will be abandoned shortly, but a number of activities carried out under the initiative will be retained. A "transversal policy note" on this topic is expected after the summer 2015. It is also expected that the innovation policy and the instruments to address the major socio-economic challenges identified in Flanders in Action will be better linked to smart specialisation and cluster policies.

Seven strategic clusters domains for smart specialisation have been identified, many of which relate to the green economy transition: sustainable chemistry, specialised manufacturing solutions, value added logistics (cluster domain providing specialised services such as recycling (reverse logistics, urban mining) or the off-shore cluster (maintenance), specialized agro-food (reduction of food waste) and an integrated building environment energy cluster.

Source: Flemish department of Economy, Science and innovation, "Policy note 12/2014 the strategic policy framework for smart specialisation in Flanders", Flanders in Action, *www.vlaandereninactie.be/over/transities.*

The new Flanders innovation policy framework under development is better linked to smart specialisation and business clusters policies. In a 2014 policy note, the Flemish department of Economy, Science and Innovation describes the evolution of the strategic policy framework for smart specialisation in Flanders and defines clusters as "geographical concentration of interrelated companies and associated institutions for research, education and training and other supporting institutions, which are active in the same or related domain of value creation. In these specific eco-systems synergies can emerge because of proximity". The objective is to develop integrated value chains in which a multitude of actors play a role. Among the various priority areas that have been identified as priorities for cluster policies, several are linked with the objective of greening the economy: for example the bio-based economy, sustainable materials management, renewable energy technology, ICT (Internet of Things, Big Data, Cloud and other Industry 4.0 domains), food and mobility.

The review of Flanders' industrial policy is therefore likely to offer additional opportunities for innovation clusters and knowledge sharing for greening the economy. The new approach gives more prominence to cross-sector and value chain clusters. This cross-sector dimension had already been explored through some projects supported by Flanders in Action such as the KRACHT project. The project was intended to assist a redesign of supply chains and address shortages in craftspeople, considering not only the needs of highly skilled workers but also of disadvantaged groups. The project developed a methodology called "local autonomous networks" that aim to enhance co-operation between value chain partners and promote innovative business solutions for industrial partners. Such cross-sectorial innovation platforms already exist at the regional level in several OECD countries – for example, the so-called "innovation theatres" in Finland or Germany.

Box 3.2. **Innovation theatres**

How can firms maximise green innovation advantage by efficiently using learning time to absorb useful messages that can promote sustainable, responsible and socially acceptable business innovations?

A new "catalyst" role for regional development agencies (RDA) or their innovation sub-sections is to organise "Innovation Theatres". This is practised in "living laboratory" settings in Finland and by public companies like *Bayern Innovativ* in Germany.

It involves a membership (cross-sectorial) of firms in the regional economy – open as needed to outside bodies and firms. It involves the RDA devoting resources for their innovation experts to design thematic "red thread" narratives that may attract a wide range of members to attend a half-day "theatre" session once every – six months. A chosen crossover and cross-sector theme might be "Living Lighter". This would appeal to the agro-food, construction, medical and metal/plastic engineering industries.

Thereafter, a "storytelling" process to fit the red thread theme would be animated by the RDA. Firms would present innovations already in practice or "white space" innovations needed but not yet created, inviting users and partners to come forward to progress their joint interest further. In this way, RDA would initiate a process of selecting from competing projects they would co-fund with partners. They (RDA), customers and suppliers would thus be "learning from among regional and outside industry and firms". Successful projects would then be owned by industrial partners. The RDA would simply take its annual membership fee.

Source: Cooke (2015).

International collaboration also plays a major role in driving innovation through value-chains and cross-sector co-operation. Flanders is very active in collaborating with international networks. For instance, it is actively involved in the European Vanguard initiative, which aims to foster collaboration across Europe on the smart specialisation roadmaps and clusters (see Box 3.3).

Box 3.3. **The Vanguard initiative: smart specialisation and European Collaboration "New growth through smart specialisation"**

The Vanguard initiative was launched in November 2013. The political leaders of 15 partner regions including Flanders gathered to sign an engagement for the industrial renaissance of Europe, calling for multi-level policy mechanisms. The objective is to align European roadmaps and priorities with regional policy tools including regional smart specialisation roadmaps and clusters. To this end, the participating regions propose to strengthen cross-border co-operation and establish a European network of pilots and demonstrators to better leverage private investments in the priority clusters. The objectives are to:

Box 3.3. **The Vanguard initiative: smart specialisation and European Collaboration "New growth through smart specialisation"** *(cont.)*

Match strategic roadmaps between regional, national and European policy levels in support of European priority areas for the future of industry. Vanguard Initiative regions are committed to developing joint roadmaps for building critical mass and complementary specialisations in these emerging industries.

Align strategic investments, arising from these roadmaps, in order to open new industrial pathways via flagship projects such as demonstrators and pilots identified in the European priority areas. Vanguard Initiative regions are committed to combining their resources with European investments in these focus areas.

Upgrade regional partnerships and clusters with global potential to European world-class clusters that can compete globally. Vanguard Initiative regions are committed to internationalising their cluster initiatives in cross-border and interregional networked European clusters and partnerships.

Source: http://era.gv.at/object/document/1268/attach/Vanguard_Initiave_2014.pdf.

The transition to a green economy is not only addressed through innovation and smart specialisation policies. Several Flemish agencies are also driving forces to promote innovation and business collaboration to address environmental challenges. For instance, in 2010 the Flanders Knowledge Centre for Water was established to bring together businesses, public authorities and research and knowledge institutions to improve water management and promote innovative demand-driven solutions.

Another example of the role of collaboration through value chains and international dimensions is the contribution of the Flemish nutrient platform to the European Phosphorus platform (see Box 3.4).

Box 3.4. **Value chain and international collaboration example: the European phosphorus platform**

Phosphorus is a non-renewable resource, non-substitutable for agriculture and food production and directly linked to global food security, as well as being important in a range of other industrial and technical uses. The world resources are finite and the European Union has listed phosphate rocks in the list of critical raw materials (materials that have a high economic importance to the EU combined with a high risk associated with their supply). At the same time, phosphorus losses pose major environmental issues. Phosphorus is the principal contributor to surface water quality failure (eutrophication) in much of Europe.

Phosphorus management in a circular loop is linked to a broad range of challenges and economic activities, including nitrogen management and other micro-nutrients, soil organic carbon, soil erosion, water treatment, food waste, contaminants, food safety and global food security. Improving the efficiency of phosphorus processing and use in industry, agriculture, livestock production, food processing and diet, and developing reuse or recovery-recycling of phosphorus can save money, contribute to reducing nutrient pollution, and create jobs in the circular economy.

To respond to the cross sector dimension of the phosphorus challenge, a Flemish nutrient platform was set up in 2012 to gather key stakeholders from the value chain including

Box 3.4. **Value chain and international collaboration example: the European phosphorus platform** *(cont.)*

phosphate mining companies, fertiliser manufacturers and distributors, agri-business sector, farmers, food producers, distributers and retailers, consumers/householders, water and sanitation service providers, policy-makers and knowledge institutes.

The Flemish nutrient platform is also collaborating with other national nutrient platforms (in particular with the Netherlands and Germany) and within the European Phosphorus Platform. This allows for broader discussions on transversal themes such as education and training and skills policies.

During the second European Sustainable Phosphorus Conference in March 2015, a session was organised in collaboration with OECD LEED to identify specific skills needed to address the phosphorus challenge. Specific skills needs were identified such as design skills (e.g. designing products in such a way that people behave in a circular way), ICT skills (e.g. in the field of precise fertilisation: 4th Industrial revolution) as well as generic skills such as transdisciplinary and communication skills. Participants concluded that pilot projects could be used to provide hands-on experience and specific training for farmers could be implemented to design better waste management practices in collaboration with NGOs.

Source: http://phosphorusplatform.eu/.

Policies connected with greening the labour market in Flanders

Employment and skills for greening the economy

With a clear mandate from high-level strategic economic policy documents, Flanders labour market policies are being reimagined for the green transition. Active labour market policies are a regional and communal competency in Flanders (see Box 3.5 below). While a large number of different actors are involved at different levels of governance, the public employment services are managed by a single Flanders wide organisation: the VDAB. Recent reforms have led to greater flexibility for VDAB offices at the local level. These reforms have enabled greater autonomy for local leaders – for example, the Antwerp district manager is able to take a leading role in forming partnerships with other local labour market actors and is responsible for local economic and sector based strategies. The VDAB has also implemented active labour market policies in Flanders to ensure that the public employment service remains responsive to the needs of the labour market (see Box 3.5).

Box 3.5. **Active labour market policy in Flanders**

Active labour market policies in Flanders

Flemish labour market policy was developed using both regional and community competences. Many topics have been covered, including diversity in the workplace, entrepreneurship, public and private labour mediation, social economy, employment measures, labour migration, sector policies and active restructuring. Flemish educational policy covers aspects related to labour market policy, such as career guidance, collaboration between the educational system and the labour market. Policy instruments and activities take many forms, and are made and delivered not only by the institutions, but also by platforms, partnerships, counsels and co-operation mechanisms.

Box 3.5. **Active labour market policy in Flanders** *(cont.)*

The management of employment services

Within Flanders, VDAB (the Flemish public employment service) offers employment services, career services, vocational training and assessment of competences, and manages the majority of Flemish labour market activation measures. Services are offered to both the unemployed and employed. The VDAB also has a responsibility for stimulating collaboration with other actors, aligning approaches and creating partnerships. Recently, VDAB has been reorganised to provide more flexibility in the management of employment policies to the local level. There is a central steering organisation and several central support services, but there is also an intermediate provincial structure being given autonomy, on top of 13 regional labour market offices. The local offices can implement and use the centrally provided measures with a certain degree of autonomy. A small proportion of their budgets can be used flexibly to support local projects covering specific local needs.

Source: OECD (2015) *Employment and skills strategies in Flanders, Belgium*, OECD Publishing, Paris.

Two reports – one prepared by Idea Consult in 2010 ("*Consequences of climate policy for the Flemish labour market*") and another prepared by the Department of Work and Social Economy (WSE) in 2011 ("*Towards a greener labour market policy: an initial policy exploration*") – provide valuable context on the thinking amongst Flemish policy makers on how to prepare the labour market for the green transition. The WSE report notes that "the transition towards a smart, sustainable and inclusive economy is doomed to fail in the absence of a well-functioning labour market". It also argues that the initial phases of the transition are expected to be particularly labour intensive. Further, skills shortages (or "problem vacancies") already exist in the labour market, may create particular problems for the green transition, and have been exacerbated recently by the ageing population. The WSE reports that technical skills shortages in particular may conceivably act as a break on the future development of green sectors and green activities. In addition, shortages in generic skills (such as safety, mobility, social skills, purposively dealing with waste, energy and raw materials) may also be problematic.

The WSE does not anticipate that many new "green" jobs will be created but rather that the focus should be on introducing sustainability strategies to existing economic sectors, and adapting and upgrading existing skills in those sectors. The public employment service in Flanders (VDAB) also notes that "in the long term all jobs are expected to become green".

The Work-and Investment plan of the previous Flemish government (2009-14) foresaw a large role for the VDAB. It is their task to develop a long-term strategy on sustainable and green growth, and to introduce sustainability principles to programmes and course activities over the next three years (WSE, 2011).The goal of the strategy is to change competences to include not only the shifting nature of current competences but also the development of new, "green", competences. This includes both technical and generic skills.

This policy was rapidly executed for the building sector. This was because "greening" education in the construction sector has a big and direct impact on other policies, including sustainable building and energy efficiency measures (WSE, 2011). The VDAB and the building sector have decided to develop a four-point strategy towards sustainable skills:

- The implementation of a "task-force" sector-VDAB, aimed at developing a common framework for action;

- The development of the VDAB building centre as a pilot case, which is responsible for co-operation with the sectors and co-ordination with other educational centres;
- The development of a course programme on energy-efficiency; and
- The development of new activities within the framework of the Work- and Investment plan.

Education and skills

Education and skills policies are also being adapted to address the skills needs emerging from the transition to a greener economy. The Flemish education system offers general education, technical education and vocational education (see Box 3.6). The Department of Education provides the main oversight to programmes provided in secondary schools, adult education centres and university colleges. Vocational training is also provided by the VDAB, which also offers courses on key competences and specific technical skills tailored to the local labour market. VDAB's vocational training and the assessment of competences is organised and managed by 87 competence centres (*competentiecentra*) grouped in 40 campuses.

Box 3.6. **The Education system in Flanders**

In Flanders, education is compulsory until the age of 18 (full-time until the age of 16). Secondary education includes three stages (two years each). After a comprehensive first stage, the second stage offers vocational options, to be completed in the third stage. The full-time track offers general education (ASO), technical education (TSO) and vocational education (BSO). The part-time track is offered by vocational secondary schools (one or two days at school and three or four days of other activities, such as labour participation (paid or unpaid work, volunteering), preparatory trajectories and bridging projects for those without the basic skills or attitudes) or personal development trajectories (intensive individual guidance for severely disadvantaged pupils).

After secondary education, many VET programmes are available in the educational system: "secondary-after-secondary" in secondary schools (Se-n-Se), associate degree programmes offered by adult education centres and university colleges, and professional bachelor programmes provided by university colleges.

Adult education centres provide skills development activities in 420 different programmes at the secondary level and the number of students enrolled has increased significantly in recent years. In 2007, programmes have been modular and can be combined with general education to lead to a diploma of secondary education (Musset, 2013). Programmes provided in secondary schools, centres for adult education, and university colleges are supervised by the Flemish Department of Education with the exception of a few vocational programmes which are under the responsibility of other ministries of the Flemish community (Musset, 2013).

Source: OECD (2015) *Employment and skills strategies in Flanders, Belgium*, OECD Publishing, Paris.

The WSE (2011) points out that climate change policy can be expected to evolve rapidly, and therefore skills policy needs to be sufficiently dynamic to keep pace. They note that the procedure for changing occupational skills profiles and competency sets to meet evolving skills needs has been very time consuming in the past and may act as a bottleneck in the future.

Flanders has been implementing a number of different initiatives to increase green skills in recent years. The Flanders Social and Economic Council (SERV) has created a new competency management system called 'Competent' along with the social partners to keep better track on evolving job profiles. The database is updated manually and informs both employment assistance (through the VDAB) and education and training curricula (through the Flanders Qualifications Framework) (see Box 3.7). Within the VDAB, matching software called ELISE also helps to best match people's skills to current and emerging jobs.

Box 3.7. **Competent occupational profile database**

The Flanders Social and Economic Council (SERV) and the Flemish Employment and Training Service (VDAB) have established an occupational profile database called Competent. It contains profiles with the details of occupations, the activities you are expected to perform and the required competencies and expertise, how the work is organised, etc. The profiles cover the entire labour market. They are classified into domains and clusters, which makes the information easy to search. The social partners are involved in the development and validation of these occupational profiles which helps in keeping them up to date. VDAB uses the database to guide job seekers, while the occupational profiles also feed into the Flemish Qualification Framework and therefore informs education and training policy.

Source: Ministry of work and the social economy (2011); *www.serv.be.*

AHOVOKS, the Flemish Agency for Higher Education, Adult Education, Qualifications and Grants, has a mission to foster quality assurance systems in both formal education projects and training. One of the most important initiatives was the Flemish Qualification Database (Vlaamse Kwalificatiestructuur, nd), which encompasses all known job qualifications and education qualifications. For each job profile a list of competences and activities is described in great detail, with the aim of including both transversal and industry-specific skills. Moreover, AHOVOKS is currently developing a project in which all existing qualification profiles in a number of sectors are screened for sustainability needs. After that, specific green skills are added to the profiles. For example, the job profile of a "roof worker" in the building sector now has the added green skill of "integration of building elements in an airtight way".

In order to recognise people's skills in greening the economy, a "green experience certificate" has been developed by the Government which recognises professional skills. It is provided on the basis of individuals being tested in the workplace and/or completing a relevant portfolio. The Social-economic council of Flanders (SERV) annually issues a call to sectorial social partners to propose professions for which such an experience certificate might be useful. The Department of Environment is also working with the Department of Education on a project to mainstream sustainability awareness across higher education curricula (see Box 3.8).

In Flanders, "sector training funds" offer training for the employed or for job-seekers aiming to work in a specific sector. These funds provide training and other types of support to employers. The provision of training and assistance is often supported through sector covenants, which are agreements between the social partners within specific economic sectors and the Flemish government. Sectoral training funds often collaborate with

Box 3.8. **Eco-campus**

Eco-campus is a project initiated by the Flemish Ministry of Environment, Nature and Energy (LNE) to promote sustainable development in higher education institutions (colleges and universities). The project is being delivered in co-operation with the Ministry of Education and Training (OV) in Flanders and Brussels. The aim is to encourage higher education institutions to educate graduates that consider sustainable development and environmental care as central frameworks for their professional and private practices. Equipping students with the necessary knowledge, skills and values will enable them to contribute to a transition to a sustainable society. The project focusses on lecturers, students and researchers as change agents. Eco-campus creates networks (e.g. learning networks, student arenas), inspires (e.g. online documentation centre with inspiring examples and useful methodologies) and supports (e.g. through pilot projects).

Source: www.lne.be/doelgroepen/onderwijs/ecocampus/literatuurmaterialen/materiaal/handleiding.pdf/view?searchterm=eco-campus.

secondary schools or post-secondary education providers in order to enhance the quality of training provided (OECD, 2015). This is important as linkages are not always optimal between the education system and the labour market, especially regarding VET streams at the secondary level (DWSE, 2011). Several of the sector covenants acknowledge the current evolution towards a more sustainable economy, including the construction workers, electricians, automotive workers, and metal workers amongst others (DWSE, 2011). Training programmes have been focused, for example, on energy performance regulations, sustainable building and renewable energy in addition to more general awareness raising.

Trade Unions are also participating in other ways on the drive for green skills. The co-operation Arbeid & Milieu (Labour and Environment) has been set up by both the trade unions and the green movement. In their view, particular attention should be raised to labour conditions (such as safety, health and job security), but also to education and training. Furthermore, they focus their attention on the availability of jobs for low-skilled workers as they often work in sectors that are vulnerable to the transition towards a green economy (Arbeid & Milieu, 2010). Training organisations co-ordinated by employers and employee organisations have also collectively set up initiatives to boost skills for the green economy, e.g. training on avoiding food waste organised by the Initiative for Vocational Training in the food industry.

Other measures include the greening of education for entrepreneurs, especially by the Flemish Agency for Entrepreneurial Education (Syntra) (WSE, 2011). Syntra is also the leading actor in the so-called "Academy for the Future", a programme which aims to provide training to the West-Flemish industry in order to catch up with ongoing transitions, such as new materials, blue energy and food.

Attention has been given to green activities in the VDAB Work Experience Program (WEP+), which aims to train the long-term unemployed (WSE, 2011). There has also been support for greening within the context of the well-developed social economy in Flanders – for example funds from both the environmental and social economy fields are invested to stimulate environmental and natural management amongst local administrations. According to DWSE (2011) 2 000 FTE workers were employed in green enterprises in the social economy sector in 2011.

International co-operation has also been set-up in the area of green skills. An example of this is the set-up of the cross-border initiative between Ghent and Terneuzen (in Belgium and the Netherlands respectively), which focusses on the "bio-based" economy (OECD, 2014b). The initiative is called Bio-Base Europe and is a joint initiative by the EU, Belgium and the Netherlands. It has been created to respond to the "need for more research and training facilities for bio-based products and processes in Europe" (OECD 2014b).

Local initiatives in Flemish provinces

Flanders consists of five provinces and 308 cities and municipalities. Cities and municipalities can cover everything that is in the interest of the collective needs of their inhabitants. However, local authorities do not receive specific funding for labour market initiatives. So-called central cities (including Antwerp and Ghent) receive contributions to support their co-ordination role in relation to the local services economy and they can use a "City Fund" to finance additional costs of regional co-ordination. Cities and municipalities usually have an alderman who is responsible for the local economy, and some also have a local employment department. As identified above, VDAB officials in larger cities such as Antwerp and Ghent also have more flexibility to engage with other actors on strategic labour market initiatives. All three of the case study areas are investing in green growth but generally through relatively ad-hoc projects.

East Flanders – Ghent

Ghent is the capital and largest city of the East Flanders province with about 250 000 inhabitants. The city is particularly engaged in the transition towards a greener economy. It introduced an action plan for sustainability – "Ghent 2020" – in 2008 and was the first Flemish city to sign the European "Covenant of Mayors" in 2009 with the objective to reduce local CO_2 emissions by at least 20% by 2020 in comparison with 2007. The project foresees the implementation of more than 105 actions and projects until 2020. A sustainable procurement strategy is integrated into this action plan. In January 2015, the Ghent city council approved the Climate Plan and a commitment to invest 105 million Euros between 2013 and 2018 in measures that directly contribute to reduced CO_2 emissions. An additional budget of 40 million Euros has been earmarked for measures that indirectly contribute to reduced emissions. Ghent has also set up a sustainable procurement strategy covering areas such as public lighting, construction, consumable goods and mobility.

Some measures of the new Climate Plan will have a direct impact on skills and jobs, such as the continuation of the "energy coaching" programmes for companies. The coaching aims to help entrepreneurs from Ghent to invest in energy efficiency or renewable energy. Following a successful pilot project, it was decided at the end of 2014 to extend the energy coaching to 110 Ghent companies. Other measures will also promote the development of sustainable business areas and a sustainable port.

The University of Ghent is also committed to developing better links between education providers and businesses to advance the green economy transition. It is currently taking part in a new Knowledge and Innovation Community on raw material financed by the European Union (see Box 3.9). This will help to link research and business, develop new curricula and promote entrepreneurship and innovation.

Another example of innovation platforms is the Ghent Living Lab that is co-ordinated by the City of Ghent. A Living Lab is a real-life test and experimentation environment where users and producers co-create innovation. The Ghent Living Lab covers areas linked

Box 3.9. **Participation in an EU knowledge and innovation community, Ghent University**

Ghent University is one of a number of Belgian universities involved in a European "knowledge and innovation community" on raw materials. This is one of a number of knowledge and innovation communities established by the European Institute of Innovation and Technology.

EIT Raw Materials is a consortium of more than 100 partners from leading businesses, research centres and universities from 20 EU Member States. The ambition is to boost the competitiveness, growth and attractiveness of the European raw materials sector via radical innovation and entrepreneurship. The collaboration across industry, academia and research in the EU is expected to:

- Support and develop over 40 incubated ideas by 2018;
- Create 16 start-ups by 2015;
- Create more than 1000 Masters and PhD EIT Label graduates by 2018; and
- Commercialise 70 patents by 2022.

One of EIT's 6 regional raw materials centres is being established in Leuven. Four core partners with operations in Flanders (Umicore, KU Leuven, Ghent University and VITO) will contribute to this project. The centre will specialise in recycling, urban mining, the recovery of metals and minerals from industrial residues, lightweight and multi-dimensional durable material design, sea floor mining and circular economy. After a transitional year in 2015, the centre is expected to be operational from the spring of 2016.

Source: University of Ghent, Flanders

to the green economy, such as "digital innovation through developing future internet enabled services for smart cities" and "green digital development including ICT enabled energy efficiency, smart energy and specific initiatives such as the Green Digital Charter". Besides the city of Ghent, the Living Lab involves several education providers such as the IBBT (Interdisciplinary Institute for Broadband Technology), the Ghent University, and University Colleges (Hogeschool Gent, Arteveldehogeschool and KaHo Sint-Lieven).

West Flanders

The West Flanders province has 1.1 million inhabitants and borders the North Sea and has important seaports (Ostend, Bruges-Zeebrugge) as well as a well-developed tourism industry. It also has a strong agro-food sector. In particular, the agro-food sector is confronted with a skills shortage due to the ageing population, the increasing outflow of skilled workers and a rather negative image which makes it difficult to attract young workers.

A shortage of technical staff (engineers and technicians) has long been identified in the province. Because of skills shortages, industries need to compete to attract and retain talent in the province. This has led to a wealth of initiatives for knowledge sharing between businesses and education providers but the green elements are not necessarily well covered in such initiatives.

For instance, new curricula (e.g. a specialised masters programme in new materials) were developed and initiatives to facilitate the transition from schools to companies were set up, such as with "visiting professionals" in schools. The regional technological centres (RTC) work as platforms to improve the connection between the education system and the labour market. These centres are co-financed by the Flemish government and companies and operate at the provincial level. In West Flanders, the RTC focuses on several industrial sectors (e.g. food industry, transport and logistics, electronics, construction). It helps to facilitate the transition from school to work by supporting internships in companies, financing didactic materials/courses and allowing students to acquire hands-on experience in a business environment.

Another initiative gathers Voka (Chamber of commerce), UNIZO, universities and colleges to carry out an awareness campaign for the agro-food industry and anchor the sector in the province. This led to development of projects such as the Flanders House of Food with a mix of company sponsoring and public funding (INTERREG, ESF, and funding from the Flemish region) (see Box 3.10).

Box 3.10. The Flanders House of Food

The Flanders' House of Food is located in Roeselare and has a visitor centre (Miummm) providing interactive and hands-on experience on dietary habits, healthy lifestyle as well as knowledge on the modern Flemish agro-food sector.

On a regular basis the Flanders' House of Food association organises **(B2B) networking events** for partners to innovatively bring together public, private and academic partners.

In the near future, this provincial site will be further developed into the **Flanders' Factory of the Future for the agro-food sector.** In addition to the Miummm, the Centre for Entrepreneurs Roeselare (starters and incubation centre for food companies) and the VDAB Training Centre for Food Professionals (e.g. packaging operators) are located on this site. Several other organizations, including research and knowledge institutes, are planning to move to this site in the near future.

Source: *www.bruns.nl/en/*.

There are also some examples of training offered by public employment services or companies related to the greening of the economy. In the construction sector, VDAB has set up a demonstration building known as the "educational house" with practical training on insulation for both employees in the construction sector and students from secondary schools. The company Bostoen has also developed its own technical eco-training. Another interesting initiative is the recent establishment of a 'Bachelor in Eco-technology' at the VIVES university college in Kortrijk, West-Flanders. The degree has a strong focus on practical training and links with industry.

A project called "the Academy of the Future" is another example of attempts to anticipate and address skills needs in the blue energy sector (offshore wind energy parks). In 2013, a lack of technical employees was identified for the sector. The "Academy of the Future" helped to map demand and supply with the input from the Flanders' maritime cluster (FMC), an interest group of large and small companies active in marine or maritime business. The project found that workers would require specific skills: language (English or German), technical, autonomy and health and safety. A new professional profile linked to offshore wind (e.g. welding for windmills) was created. The Academy collaborated with Syntra West and university colleges as well as with private trainers. Trainings will start next April-May 2015, provided the overarching policy framework promoting off-shore wind (Plan Stevin) is implemented.

Antwerp

The province is a strong economic centre in Flanders with a population of 1.8 million. The Port of Antwerp is the economic heart of the province and also has a strong industrial base. The province is also home to the University of Antwerp and research centres such as the European Institute for Reference Materials and Measurements (IRMM) and the Flemish Institute for Technological Research (VITO).

The city and province are promoting sustainability through their work. The Port of Antwerp started sustainability reporting in 2012. This initiative started as part of a "Total Plan for a More Competitive Port" launched in 2010 in response to the global financial crisis. To implement the plan, port authorities gathered all stakeholders to draw up a joint vision for sustainability and make sustainability a new competitive advantage of the port (Sustainable Port of Antwerp, nd).

The City of Antwerp and the Flemish Region are also working together to turn the old Petroleum South site, a site once dedicated to the refining of petroleum products, into an industrial park called "Blue Gate Antwerp" with strong green elements. The site will be developed according to the principles of eco-effectiveness – a new way of economic thinking that is based on closing cycles and avoiding waste or reusing it as a raw material for another process. It is also the city's ambition to become an "international pathfinder for renewable sources of energy".

There are also initiatives related to skills for sustainability focusing on specific sectors. In Antwerp, VDAB is collaborating with Umicore, a global materials technology and recycling giant to organise training on recycling and material reuse for future "Material Technology Operators". In addition, VDAB is currently exploring the concept of 3D-printing and how to best incorporate this technology in training programmes.

In addition to the local dimension, Antwerp is also home to the International Centre for Corporate Learning on Business Ethics & Sustainability (Antwerp ITTCO) set up in 2012 to provide courses on sustainable development, corporate social responsibility and business ethics. The Centre is affiliated with UNITAR, the United Nations Institute for Training and Research. It also involves the diamond sector in Antwerp (Antwerp World Diamond Centre and Fonds voor Diamantnijverheid) and CIBJO (*World Jewellery Confederation* in Milan), with the support of the City of Antwerp and the Flemish Government and in close collaboration with local and international businesses, trade unions, academia and NGOs. Initial activities currently focus on the international diamond and jewellery industry but the scope of courses will expand to other sectors in the future.

Conclusions

The policy framework of Flanders clearly recognises the strategic importance of greening skills and jobs and fostering green innovation. In particular, public agencies such as VDAB and AHOVOKS have well integrated green elements.

There is a wealth of initiatives in place in Flanders at the regional, provincial and city level to gear up the employment and skills system to boost the transition towards a green economy. In addition, many knowledge-sharing platforms for businesses and involving the education sector do exist although the green element is not always prominent (e.g. for the food cluster in West Flanders).

These local initiatives are not always aware of each other and may lack the critical mass to make a significant impact. The multiplication of initiatives could also undermine business participation, as it may be difficult to identify where resources are best placed.

References

Antwerp ITCCO (2015), *www.unitar.org/antwerp-itcco/* (accessed 18 February 2015).

Arbeid & Milieu (2010), *Green jobs, http://groenejobs.be/uploads/Documenten/am_2010_3_katern.pdf* (accessed 18 December 2014).

Blue Gate Antwerp (2015), *www.bluegateantwerp.eu/en/what* (accessed 18 February 2015).

Empirica (2014) *e-Skills in Euoprea: Belgium Country Report, http://eskills-monitor2013.eu/fileadmin/monitor2013/documents/Country_Reports/Country_Report_Belgium_th.pdf* (accessed 20 October 2015).

Flemish House of Food (2015), *www.miummm.be/en/about-miummm/* (accessed 18 February 2015).

Gent (2015), *Ghent Climate Plan 2014-2019, https://stad.gent/ghent-international/city-policy-and-structure/ghent-climate-plan-2014-2019* (accessed 18 February 2015).

Government of Flanders (2014). *The Strategic Policy Framework for Smart Specialization in Flanders.* Department of Economy, Science and Innovation.

Government of Flanders, Flemish department of Economy, Science and innovation, "Policy note 12/2014 the strategic policy framework for smart specialisation in Flanders", Flanders in Action *www.vlaandereninactie.be/over/transities* (accessed on 20 October 2015).

Government of Flanders Departement Leefmilieu, Natuur en Energie. (2015). *Decade of Education for Sustainable Development in Flanders: Current Assessment*, Vlaamse Overheid.

Government of Flanders, Department of Work and Social Economy (2011) "*Towards a greener labour market policy: an initial policy exploration*".

Government of Flanders, Kwalificatiedatabank 2010, *http://vlaamsekwalificatiestructuur.be/kwalificatiedatabank/* (accessed on 20 October 2015).

OECD (2010) *Cluster Policies.* OECD Innovation Policy Platform.

OECD (2012). *Draft Synthesis Report on Innovation Driven-Growth in Regions: The Role of Smart Specialisation*, OECD Publishing, Paris.

OECD LEED (2005), *Business Clusters: Promoting Enterprise in Central and Eastern Europe*, OECD Publishing, Paris.

Port of Antwerp (2015), *www.portofantwerp.com/en/sustainability* (accessed 18 February 2015).

Sleeckx, E. (2014) *Beleidsnota Economie & Innovatie*, Vlammse Regering.

Sustainable Port of Antwerp (nd) *Sustainable cooperation for a sustainable future, www.sustainableportofantwerp.com/en* (accessed 18 February 2015).

Vlaamse Regering (2014), *Werk, Economie, Wetenschap en Innovatie*, Vlaamse Regering. Vlaams minister van Werk, Economie, Innovatie en Sport.

Vlaamse Kwalificatiestructuur (nd), *Kwalificatiedatabank www.ond.vlaanderen.be/kwalificatiestructuur/kwalificatiedatabank/* (accessed 18 February 2015).

Chapter 4

Greening company practices in Flanders

This chapter examines sector-specific practices in three major industries in Flanders, namely the agro-food, building and chemicals sectors, with respect to building green skills and promoting long-term and sustainable green practices. Primary evidence on the priorities in each industry are examined with reference to perceptions of current and future skills needs.

While government and local initiatives are in place to foster the green economy transition in Flanders, the private sector also has a key role to play. How are companies envisaging the green economy transition in Flanders? What is the perceived impact on employment and skills? What are the emerging strategies to address skills needs and gaps? In response to these questions, several important sectors of Flanders' economy have been selected for in-depth review: the building, chemicals and agro-food sector. The building sector is a labour intensive sector with a high potential for transformation in the whole province. The chemicals sector has a significant presence in the economy of Antwerp, whilst the agro-food sector is prominent in West Flanders.

This chapter captures the findings of OECD LEED desk research, interviews with industry federations and individual companies (the list of interviewed companies is available in Annex I) as well as a company survey.

Sector specific initiatives to green practices

The building sector: a clear regulatory pathway to green the sector until 2021 facilitates the identification of skills needs and the skills ecosystems response

A strong labour-intensive sector of the economy in Flanders

The building sector is characterised by a multitude of activities, such as raw material extraction, building materials manufacturing, the actual construction of houses, inside installations, and all kinds of services that are linked to all those activities. In 2010, the Belgian building sector generated a turnover of 47.7 billion euro, of which 66 per cent was from Flanders (IDEA Consult, 2011). The building sector is very labour-intensive: personnel costs count for 70 per cent of the total costs, whilst the other 30 per cent can be attributed to material costs. The building sector is also very dependent on manual labour, especially on construction sites (IDEA Consult, 2011). In Flanders, the construction sector mainly consists of small and middle-sized enterprises that are mostly active on a local level.

A green strategy boosted by regulation and a clear pathway to link environmental and training policies

The demand for more sustainable products and services create important market opportunities. This has been strongly stimulated by the Energy Performance Building Directive (EPBD) of the European Union, which has been implemented in national legislation and is rather progressive by European standards. Apart from that, financial stimulation measures and campaigns make sure that consumers and companies are inclined to invest in energy efficiency and renewable energy measures (WSE 2011), although these subsidies have been significantly reduced since 2014. The building sector is also a crucial actor in climate change activities: as the energy use per square meter of housing in Belgium exceeds the European average, many opportunities for energy efficiency and emission reduction can be traced to the building sector.

The sector is therefore an interesting case study for assessing the employment and skills impact of the green economy transition as it benefits from a clear regulatory framework and pathway until 2021. The regulatory predictability is very helpful for economic sectors envisaging long terms trends, investments and skills developments. This also facilitates better linkages between environmental policies and training provisions, as was the case in France (see Box 4.1 below).

Box 4.1. **Linking environmental policies and training provisions – the example of construction in France**

The skills of construction workers is often pointed out as a possible weak link in the implementation of building codes introduced to improve the energy efficiency of housing and commercial buildings. France introduced a certification system with a specific label for companies that conducted specific training of their staff on energy efficiency (a unique label indicating that professionals have been trained to deliver environmental quality "Environmental Guarantee Recognition", RGE label). Several public awareness campaigns run by the French Energy agency ADEME were carried out encouraging consumers to call for trained professionals with RGE labels. Since 2014, public financial assistance for renovating buildings is conditioned to the employment of RGE labelled companies (so-called eco-conditionality). In 2008, France also launched a programme of continuous vocational training partly financed with a contribution of EDF with white certificates called FEEBAT. Between 2008 and 2012, the scheme trained 48 000 construction professionals. The programme has been extended to 2017.

Source: OECD 2015 forthcoming.

Skills and employment impact of the transition to a green economy: new jobs and skills

The sector offers opportunities for new jobs and for upgrading skills in existing jobs. This is boosted significantly by the widespread acceptance of green building standards. New jobs and new skills have arisen. Airtight building, cavity wall insulation, new approaches to ventilation and the use of energy experts (EPB and EPC) are new developments in the industry. There is also more PV, underfloor heating and wall heating. However, old jobs require new skills because each worker must play their part in the value chain. This applies to practically all jobs and all parts of the value chain. Next to the construction of new buildings, more jobs have been created for the maintenance of the house and its equipment (e.g. heating devices).

The Flemish Building Confederation (VCB) estimates that policy initiatives concerning water treatment, soil remediation and recycling have created 8 000 new jobs, which is expected to grow to 24 000 jobs in 2020 (IDEA Consult, 2011). The need for skills training for several job profiles has also been acknowledged by a survey of the Flemish Building Confederation. Because of changing legislation, a need for more training has arisen: 57 per cent of all companies expect more stringent regulation to lead to a need for training of new techniques and an adaptation of building practices (IDEA Consult, 2011).

The need for skilled personnel has increased dramatically in the building sector. Nearly all jobs in the sector require more technical and more complex skills than before. The problem of finding staff with the right skills tends to be more significant for SMEs, which comprise the majority of construction companies in Flanders. As a result, the importance of both pre-career training and training of workers has gone up significantly.

A response of the skills and education system

In this context, training activities are proving crucial to adapt the sector to a green economy. The sector is currently collaborating with a wide range of training providers to address skills needs. The objective is not only to better equip future recruits through initial education but also to ensure the training of the current workforce.

The Flemish Building Confederation (VCB) organises annual congresses on this issue as well as specific training, many of which are organised at the provincial level. The public training providers such as the VDAB and Syntra agencies are also important players. VDAB has set up a Sustainable Building Task Force together with the construction and wood sector and their social partners: the construction employers federation and several education and technical organisations. This Task Force developed a strategic plan for the construction industry in 2020 that identifies skills for nearly zero energy construction (insulation, ventilation, air-tight building, timber frame, renewable energy, sustainable renovation and green roofs).

The construction sector is also collaborating with university colleges through a wide range of activities such as a "roadshow" at university colleges and the development of a professional Bachelor of Building (IDEA Consult 2011). New trajectories have been initiated that look at new techniques or add a module on energy efficiency, often conducted in partnership with the sector. Examples of this include:

- An education trajectory towards "Energy co-ordinator" of the Association KU Leuven and university colleges, which aims at training architects and contractors;
- A modular training scheme set up by Cevora (a joint paritair committee of employers and trade unions for the building sector and the Flemish Building Confederation);
- A modular training scheme in "energy efficient building", comprised of several technical skills including handling condensation boilers, heat pumps, solar energy. (IDEA Consult, 2011).

Most stakeholders interviewed consider on-going training initiatives and the response of the skills ecosystems adequate to respond to the sector's emerging skills needs. Nevertheless, some green frontrunner companies are still choosing to develop skills in-house to stay ahead of the market and develop a competitive advantage.

The chemicals sector: the sector is increasingly aware of the need to transition towards a green economy but has difficulties finding the highly technical skills it needs.

The chemical sector: a traditionally strong sector in Flanders increasingly aware of the need to transition to a green economy

Since the 1960s and due to the substantial development of the harbour, Antwerp has developed a strong chemical sector. Continuous investment from both Belgian and international sources has transformed the petrochemical sector and other chemical subsectors into a world-class petrochemical cluster. The turnover of the chemical industry in Belgium was 38.8 billion euro (2008), particularly due to a rise in the pharma and biotech industries. However, the petrochemical industry remains the most important chemical industry in the cluster (IDEA Consult, 2011).

The chemical industry in Flanders has seen the development of several initiatives aimed at making the industry more sustainable. An important initiative in the industry is

FISCH – Chemistry for Sustainability. FISCH aims to identify, stimulate and catalyse innovations for sustainable chemistry in Flanders by supporting companies in the start-up of innovation projects (FISCH 2014).

A sector facing skills shortage in highly technical skills

Growing skills demand in all occupations and profiles has increased in response to innovation, strict and growing legislation and the quest for cost reductions. This trend is only partly due to the transition to a green economy although skills related to the green economy are becoming an important component. One interviewee explained that the company needed "people that have sustainable chemistry in their DNA".

A structural shortage of employees with a technical background has been identified in the sector. On the one hand, there is a rising demand for highly specialised skills for which training does not exist. On the other hand, there is also a growing need for interdisciplinary skills, such as an agronomist with knowledge of biochemistry or applied mathematics. These profiles are hard to find on the labour market.

Skills ecosystem response: collaboration to build a talent pipeline

The sector federations have set up a wide range of activities and collaborations to address these skills shortages and also to improve the attractiveness of the sector.

Essenscia and Federplast, the sector federations for the chemical and plastics sector, have undertaken activities to increase the visibility and attractiveness of jobs in the sector. They have published a website that can be used by teachers in order to inform their students on jobs in the sector. Another important project is the covenant on chemical industry and education, which has been set up by Essenscia, the trade unions, the Flemish government and school systems (Essenscia, 2012). The goal of this initiative is twofold: the initiative aims to both increase the influx of young people into the chemicals sector and deepen the relationship between the sector and school systems. This should be done by 1) improving the sector "branding" for the teachers and the students, 2) improving the influx of students or young adults from studies other than chemistry, and 3) intensifying the current co-operation between the chemical sector and the education system. Additionally, the sector organizes job fairs, called "We are Chemistry", which invites the 20 biggest chemical companies to present their sector in order to bring them into contact with last year students and unemployed jobseekers.

Companies in the sector are also pursuing several strategies to cope with the skills issue. Many companies collaborate with universities and university colleges. Activities include inviting university professors to discuss specialised curricula development, taking part in guest lectures, conducting school visits to companies and holding student competitions such as the Footsteps project. Although this collaboration strategy works and effectively leads to the take-up of relevant expertise in the curricula, the expectations towards the training and education sector are "realistic". The industry's focus is on attracting employees with more and better general technical skills. On the other hand, the sector believes that specialised technical skills and expertise are best developed through on-the-job training and should not be expected from the training system. One interviewee explained: "Due to the shortage of technically-skilled employees, we focus more on a creative mind-set than on specific skills. Internal trainings do the rest". Some training courses, such as process operator training, are organized by sector federations, or the employment agency VDAB.

The sector is also indirectly benefitting from the region's activities to attract students to STEM (Science, Technology, Engineering and Mathematics) curricula and careers. In 2012, the Flemish government launched a STEM action and a science communication plan for this purpose. In 2014, one-quarter of the 308 Flemish municipalities had set up a STEM academy, a network of organisations that organise after-school activities around science and technology for children and youngsters up to 18 years old.

The agro-food sector shows limited awareness of the need to address the transition to a green economy: the sector does not anticipate major skills changes related to greening its practices

The Belgian agrofood sector consists of 4 800 companies who buy resources from farmers or other food companies (Fevia, 2014). The food industry is the biggest employer in Belgium and employs 88 700 workers. The turnover in the Flemish agricultural sector was estimated to be 5.1 billion euro in 2011. The products with the greatest contribution to this number were pork (27 %), dairy products (14%), beef (13%) and vegetables (11%) (MIRA-AMS, 2012).

The sector still faces significant challenges in the transition towards a green economy such as the limited corporate environmental awareness of the sector and its value chain, e.g. cleaning services, packaging or supermarkets. There is also a tendency to think mainly in "economies of scale" with processes that cheapen products but do not consider green issues (Cooke 2015).

In recent years, several new initiatives and organizations working on sustainability and the greening of the sector have emerged. One of these initiatives is Flanders' Food. Flanders' Food aims to be a "unique, strategy-driven platform that contributes through innovation to a more competitive, innovative and sustainable agro-food industry" (Flanders' Food, 2014).

Skills needs are generally not regarded as an important challenge in the Flemish agro-food sector. The food industry has its own training institute: the "Initiative for Professional Training in the Food Sector", (Initiatieven voor Professionele Vorming van de Voedingsnijverheid, IPV). IPV is financed by companies of the sector through a "training fee" of 0.2% of total labour costs. Employers and employee organizations each have half of the seats in the board and the general assembly of IPV.

Training is generally not perceived as a major obstacle. Today the sector has no major problems in finding skilled personnel and no "green skills wave has been experienced yet". The sector does not expect new types of green jobs or skills to arise in the near future. However, it expects that current employees will need more and new skills in the future. Finding good people with the right skills is a challenge in the sector due to complexity, increasing specialization and skills inflation, rather than due to green elements. The need for skills increases as employees are given more integrated tasks. Jobs with technical skills are also undergoing change that is mostly dealt with inside the companies. Highly-skilled agricultural engineering specialising in green growth methods is not new but has grown increasingly important.

When asked for their green skills development strategies, the response of the surveyed companies' is that they do not view green skills as a strategic priority. Collaboration with sector federations does exist for some, rather general, skills, such as leadership and legislation. Specific training is conducted with private training companies, but on-the-job training remains the most important strategy. The sector has only limited collaboration with the education sector for skills related to sustainability, largely through working with bachelor's and master's thesis students and interns.

Although the Flanders food initiative is not focusing specifically on skills development, it does aim to improve scientific and technological knowledge at the company-level (SMEs in particular), and to improve the knowledge transfer to companies to effectively develop new and/or improved products and processes (Flanders' Food, 2014).

Conclusions

Interviews with business federations and companies tend to show that the construction, chemicals and agro-food sectors are transitioning to a greener Flanders economy at differing paces. In the construction sector, a stable and predictable regulatory framework has helped identify skills needs and gaps and the education and training system response has adapted its response to companies' needs. The chemicals industry has started recognising the importance of sustainability in the training of workers but has difficulty finding the highly technical and multidisciplinary skills it needs. Collaboration between the sector and the education and training system is mainly focused on building a talent pipeline. The agro-food sector has limited awareness of the green economy transition. It is not currently anticipating major changes related to skills for greening its practices.

Company survey

A company survey was conducted in October 2014 to complement the analysis and the interviews with sector federations and individual companies and better understand the reality of business practices in relation to the greening of the economy. Around 1 500 companies from four sectors – agriculture, food manufacturing, chemical industry and construction – were contacted by phone and 100 responded to the survey. Although the sample of companies is not statistically robust in view of the high number of companies operating in the selected sectors, the company survey gives useful indications of company perceptions.

The large majority of Flemish companies have taken first steps to green their business

Flemish companies are aware that the transition to a greening economy is ongoing and 82% of companies interviewed claim to have introduced "green measures". Half of them have introduced a small number of measures and less than 10% affirm to have completely reshaped their businesses.

This highlights that some companies have developed proactive strategies to accompany and foster this transition, while others are more passive. The interviews bring forward a mixed picture: on the one hand, many activities relating to the greening of the economy are taking place in and around companies, but on the other hand, many activities are found in a relatively limited group of frontrunners. However the majority of companies are still lagging behind, and are not fully aware of the importance of the green transition.

When asked about the most important environmental challenges for their businesses, companies in Flanders frequently mention energy, waste management and raw material efficiency as major challenges. There are slight differences between economic sectors and companies in agriculture also mention challenges related to water use and water quality.

The majority of companies have at least taken a number of first steps towards tackling environmental challenges. As shown in the figure below, more than 90% of firms that

Figure 4.1. **Perceived environmental challenges**

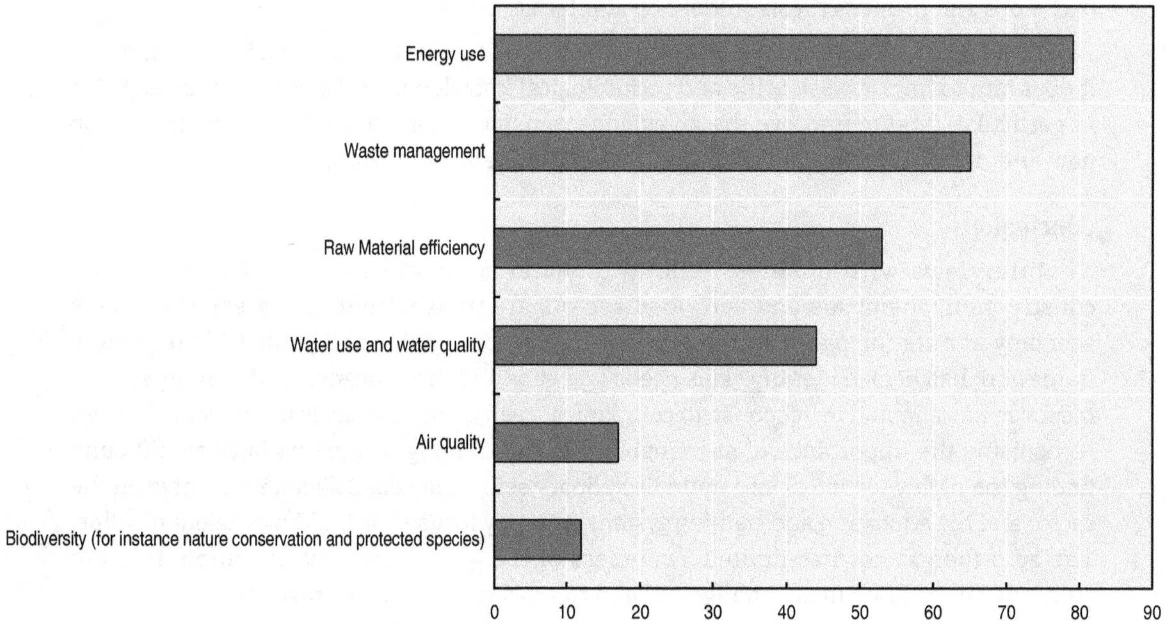

Source: OECD LEED company survey.

Table 4.1. **Perceived environmental challenges by sector**

Sector	Most prominent challenge	Second most prominent challenge
Agriculture	Energy use	Water use and quality
Manufacturing of food products	Energy use	Waste management
Chemical industry	Energy use	Waste management, raw material efficiency
Construction	Waste management	Energy use

Source: OECD LEED company survey.

implemented green measures have done so in relation to waste management, including waste reduction and recycling. Around 80% of companies have implemented measures related to energy efficiency and renewable energy, pollution reduction, or water efficiency and water quality. Half of the respondents even report to have taken actions to conserve nature. Next to the topical analysis, companies report greening initiatives in all parts of activities and all phases of the value chain: product design, processes, services, staff operations, logistics and waste management. A practical example of the greening process undertaken by an existing business is the sugar refinery of Tienen (see Box 4.2).

Complying with regulation but also with the vision of senior management are the most important drivers for companies in Flanders to green their businesses

The main driver for green companies appears to be environmental regulation on waste and water quality. A number of companies referred explicitly to the EU Emission Trading Scheme (ETS), REACH and energy performance regulation in the construction sector.

The second driver was the vision of the CEO. Indeed, companies with a Director who firmly believes in the opportunity and the necessity of a greener economy can make a large difference. This conclusion is interesting, as it opens doors for recommendations towards more emphasis on environmental issues in business schools. Compatibility with the

Figure 4.2. **Green measures implemented by Flemish companies**

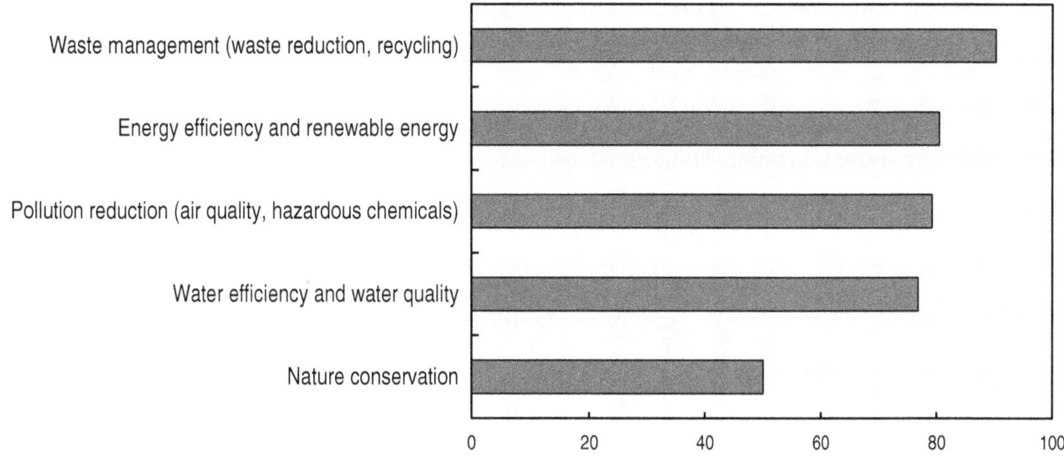

Source: OECD LEED company survey.

Box 4.2. **Greening practices in a sugar refinery**

The Sugar Refinery of Tienen is a Belgian company founded in 1836, producing sugar and related products. Using sugar beets as the source for its production, it produces 486 235 tons of sugar per year. It sells its products both to consumers and industrial clients.

As its main production facility in Tienen is located in the city centre, the company has a long tradition in mitigating the negative impacts of its activities. Using people, planet and profit as its guiding principle, the Sugar Refinery of Tienen implements a number of actions, such as regulations on transport, energy use, CO_2-reduction and waste management.

"During the harvest period (September to January), our sugar plants produce more energy than they consume, thanks to our residual biomass flows. Moreover, our entire production process, from sugar beet to sugar, is entirely waste-free, as all the residual flows go back to agriculture, resulting in a closed loop. Even the water coming from our beets is 100% re-used for washing the beets, also resulting in a closed water loop."

Source: Tiense Suiker, *www.tiensesuikerraffinaderij.com/nl-BE/Hoe-we-werken/Milieubeleid.*

values of the firm, improving the image and cost savings are also perceived as important drivers for greening the business.

There was less agreement on the capacity of greening in relation to new business opportunities. The believers, which represent around 40% of the companies interviewed, stress the importance of being a first mover as a condition for a business case. Along the same line, there seems to be doubt as to whether the consumer is demanding greener products and businesses. It seems that, although on the rise, consumers' demand for greening is still only concentrated with a minority of consumers. Concomitant with that observation, some stakeholders mentioned that sustainable consumption, e.g. organic food, still has not gone beyond the niche level. Another remark made on this point is that the pressure from consumers is larger with but not limited to business-to-customer (B2C) companies. Business-to-business (B2B) companies reported that the pressure of the consumer is transferred upwards in the value chain: B2B are pressured by their B2C customers, so the pressure for greening is both direct and indirect.

Finally, pressure by NGOs or local stakeholders is less influential in promoting greening initiatives. Of course, large individual differences can occur. One manufacturing company that is located in the centre of a city emphasised in an interview that this had been a very important driver for greening.

For companies who have not introduced green measures in their business, the identified drivers remain similar. The surveyed companies that had not begun the greening process report that consumer demand as a relatively more important factor than companies that had already introduced green measures into their businesses (see Box 4.3).

Figure 4.3. **Main drivers to green businesses**

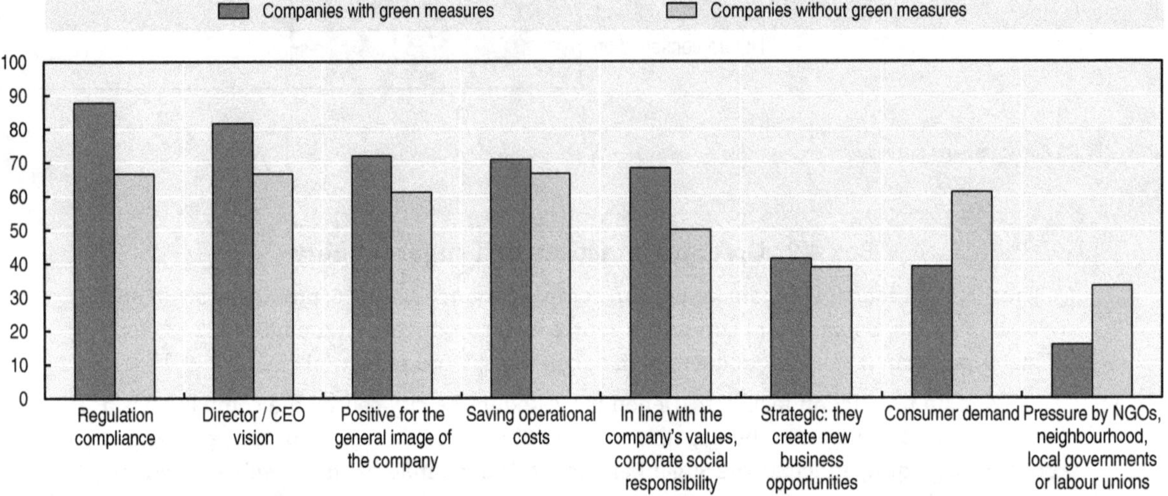

Source: OECD LEED company survey.

Box 4.3. **What's driving the change towards greener company practices?**

Market demand as a driver – Taminco

Taminco is a global chemical company, with a focus on niche markets. It is a leading producer of alkylamines & derivatives and a major producer of formic acid & derivatives. Its customers are in the manufacture products for the agriculture, animal nutrition, water treatment, personal & home care and oil & gas end-markets. Environmental care is one of Taminco's three core values. It is translated in a set of quantified 2020 goals in the following areas: green solvents, more efficient and renewable animal feed, bio-stimulant products, CO_2, waste, NO_x, water usage, water quality, logistics and sustainable behaviour.

One of the drivers for their greening strategy is market demand:

"The market is one of the drivers to green our business. Even as a business to business company, the value chain transfers consumer's demand for greening through the value chain: some of our clients are companies that sell to consumers, so they pass on demands regarding sustainability to us."

A strong CEO vision for sustainability – Bostoen

Bostoen was a classical building company until 2007. Then the family's son took over as the CEO, and his vision completely changed the vision of the company. It soon decided to focus on passive houses primarily. It is a good example of how important a visionary the CEO can be as a driver for the greening of a business. Today, the portfolio of the company has been diversified again, but energy neutrality and passive houses remain at the core of the activities. The company illustrates that it pays to go for the first-mover-advantage: it was already prepared for the nearly-energy-neutral standard, imposed by the European Union by 2021, before it was even approved.

Box 4.3. **What's driving the change towards greener company practices?** *(cont.)*

"Based on a strong vision on society and sustainability, our new CEO decided in 2007 to give passive houses a central place in our product portfolio. As a result, our staff needed a partial skills switch, in which accuracy is as central as specific technical skills. 80% of the skills were only there, 20% change was then necessary, and implemented. Back then, I temporarily took on the job of trainer to upskill the whole staff of our company. Nowadays, every new employee gets a short training course and the rest of the required skills are taught on the job." (quote from the interview).

Source: OECD LEED Boosting skills for greener jobs – Interviews.

The lack of funding as well as administrative/legal barriers are perceived as major obstacles to green businesses

It is clear that some obstacles for greening in Flemish companies exist. Several stakeholders and companies mentioned that the economic crisis has forced companies to cut back on other engagements, such as greening activities not directly linked to their core activities. Figure 4.4 shows that high cost is perceived as the main obstacle by the respondents of the survey. Administration and legal barriers are also important, while the lack of partnership opportunities, employees' skills and the lack of consumer demand have a lower impact on the capacity of greening businesses.

Figure 4.4. **Perceived obstacles to green businesses in Flanders**

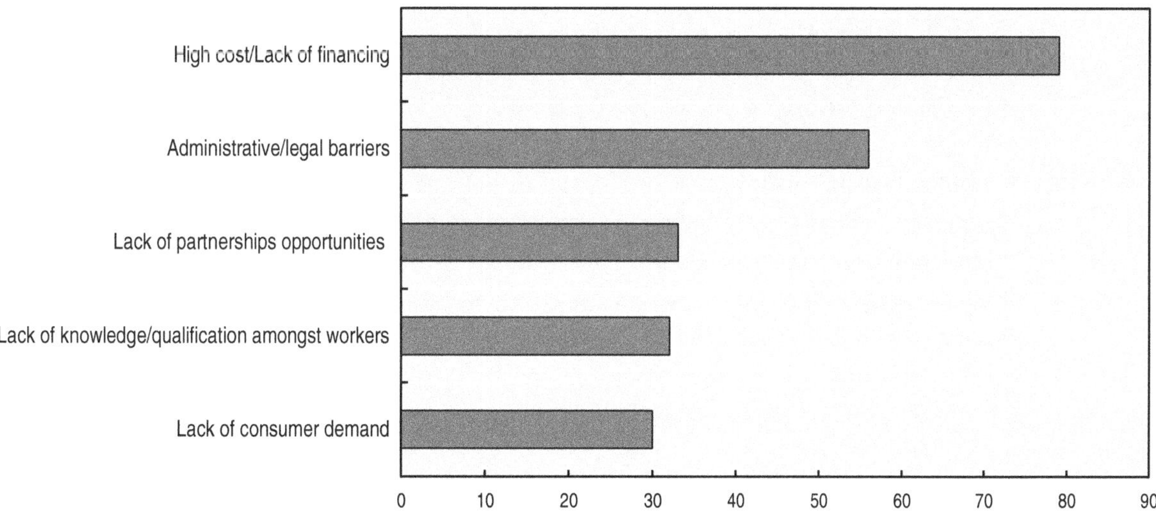

Source: OECD LEED company survey.

In this context, legislation and regulation compliance is not only an important driver for greening, but also for skills development and training provision. The development of training programmes for the professionals issuing energy performance certificates for buildings is a good example. This new occupation is legally defined. With this legal framework, there is an incentive and a market for offering training programmes for energy auditors/certifiers, which guarantees an inflow of subscribers. Legislation can thus have a positive effect on the development of new training for green skills.

The green transition is having an impact on skills, and mainly on technical skills

Among firms that have introduced "green measures", 70% had to address skills related issues. In order to have the skills necessary to green businesses, more than half of the firms had to upskill or retrain current staff, while a third needed to hire external consultants and less than 10% hired new staff. A wider range of skills practices were also identified during company interviews (see Box 4.4).

Box 4.4. **Company skills practices**

When interviewed, companies pointed to a number of skills strategies they use to have a workforce equipped with the skills they need for the transition to a green economy. Notably, these practices do not differ widely from common HR practices.

- Building a talent pipeline (ensure that education and training prepare future workers with appropriate skills)
  - Collaboration with the education sector (school visits, higher education)
  - Improve attractiveness of the firm for trainees
  - Baekelantmandaat: Ph. d in collaboration with university
- Recruitment
  - Send job vacancies to universities or faculties.
  - Send job vacancies to specific professors and academics.
- Training
  - Collaboration with public and private training providers, strengthen linkages with sector federation trainings
  - Hire specialised consultants to train the employee(s)
  - Establish mentors within the company: experienced employees train less experienced colleagues;
- Knowledge sharing networks
  - Encourage employee participation in thematic conferences
  - Collaboration with other companies in the sector, or with companies in the value chain.
  - Collaboration with Flemish government, e.g. Innovation projects; KMO-umbrella (a scheme that provides subsidies to SMEs including for training activities)

Source: OECD LEED – individual company interviews.

The lack of technical skill is highlighted by firms participating in the survey. The gap with other types of occupations is remarkable indicating that sales and customer services, administrative, legal and management occupations do not represent a significant obstacle for companies to become greener.

The lack of technical skill is also confirmed by interviews with Flemish industry representatives. They frequently mention the difficulty of finding employees with a (general) technical background; this is true for both high (e.g. engineers) and low (e.g. mechanics) skills profiles regardless of the sector of activity and the firm size.

When looking at the skills needed to green the business, the difference between the categories are less pronounced. Technical skills are needed in 76% of firms followed by communication and interpersonal skills (58%) and entrepreneurial skills (48%).

Figure 4.5. **Types of occupations needed to further develop green measures**

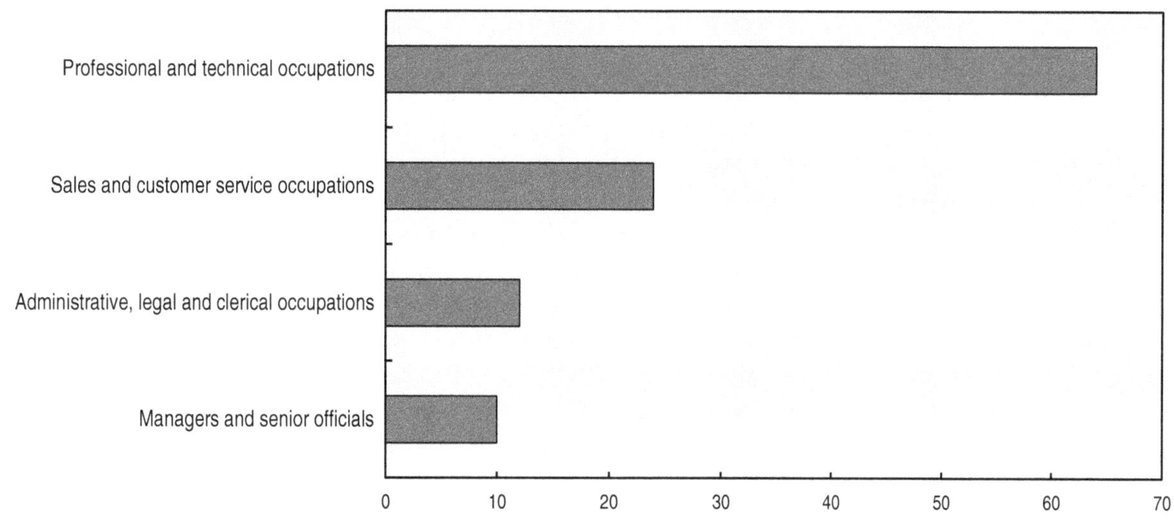

Source: OECD LEED company survey.

Figure 4.6. **Skills needed to further develop green measures**

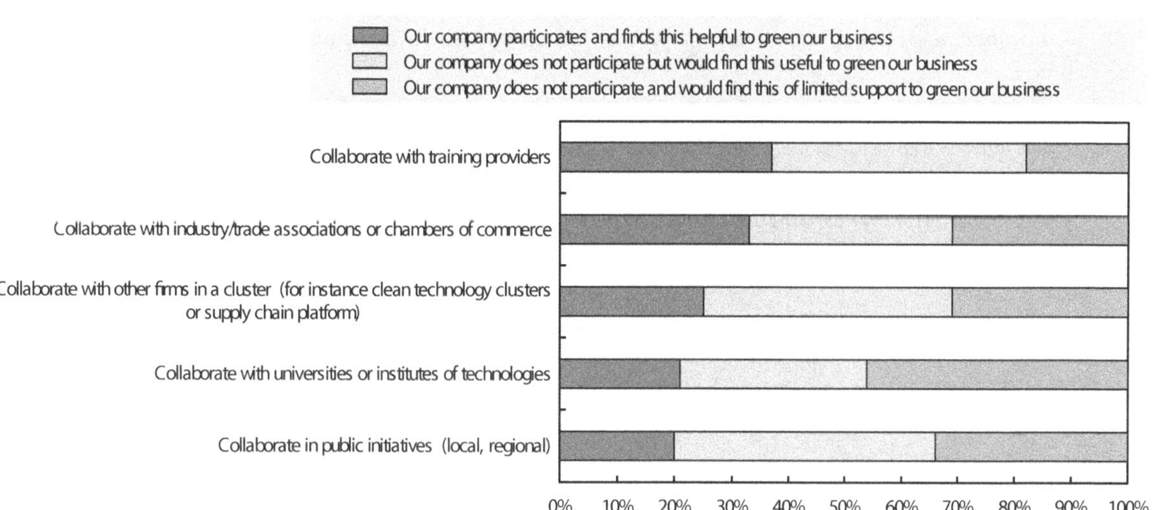

Source: OECD LEED company survey.

The business representatives interviewed also notice an evolution towards integrated tasks: employees should not only master their own part of the value chain, but also the activities that come before and after theirs (see Box 4.5).

Several interviewees believe that skills related to sustainability should be present in all occupational profiles and at all skill levels. In order to build these skills, notions of sustainability and the role of green measures should be included in education programmes and trainings more often. These will contribute to the creation of a mind-set to make the future workforce more creative and innovative and more aware of green issues.

Skills ecosystem and knowledge- sharing activities

Knowledge-sharing activities could be a useful tool to assist firms in greening their business. The number of companies that are actually involved in this type of activities is

Box 4.5. **The importance of "integrated" skills profiles**

INEOS

INEOS is a multinational that produces petrochemicals, specialty chemicals and oil products. In Belgium, the company has 6 production facilities and one research lab, where intermediaries, plastics and specialty chemicals are produced.

As other chemical companies, INEOS has a range of internal policies to mitigate environmental impacts e.g. by reducing its energy intensity, material input and transportation activities. It also contributes to the development of new environmentally friendly products, such as carbon fibre. "*In the past years, we have been able to further improve our material efficiency. In 2007, we needed 1 025 kg of monomer to produce one tonne of polymer; currently, this input is down to 1 006 kg per tonne.*" (quote from the interview).

INEOS has found that integrated skills profiles are increasingly important: "Engineers have a large impact in our business. We are increasingly looking for engineers with more than just production skills, we want people who have ideas, are creative. That (partly technical) creativity is becoming more important than specific technical skills. Sustainability is one aspect where that creativity can play, but not the only one" (quote from the interview.)

Taminco

Taminco, a global chemical company, also insists on the integration of several science fields.

"The transition to a green economy shifts our skills needs towards more integrated science domains. The narrow scientist who has no knowledge about adjacent fields is increasingly being replaced by multidisciplinary profiles with knowledge that concerns a large part of the value chain."

Source: OECD LEED 2014 – Boosting skills for greener jobs interview.

not high, but many are interested in being part of one in the future. One reason could be that the respondents of the survey are mainly small and micro companies that often lack financial resources and staff to take part in these extra activities. This is in contrast with our interviews, which were generally larger companies that are more actively using knowledge-sharing strategies.

As shown in Figure 4.7, companies seem to collaborate mainly with training providers, industry associations and the chambers of commerce. Participation in public initiatives both at the local and regional level is less common.

Training provision and obstacles to green skills development

More than a third (37%) of the companies participating in the survey collaborate with training providers and another 45% would find that useful. Figure 4.9 shows the most common training providers that offer green skills training to Flemish companies.

Trade and industry associations are the most commonly used training providers (70%). This can be explained by the fact that providing training to their members is one of their key competencies. Private training providers (63%) and VDAB (54%) are also often used for training purposes by firms. Other parts of the same enterprise, chambers of commerce and the universities are less commonly used. Trade unions are not frequently mentioned as training providers.

Figure 4.7. **Participation in knowledge-sharing activities**

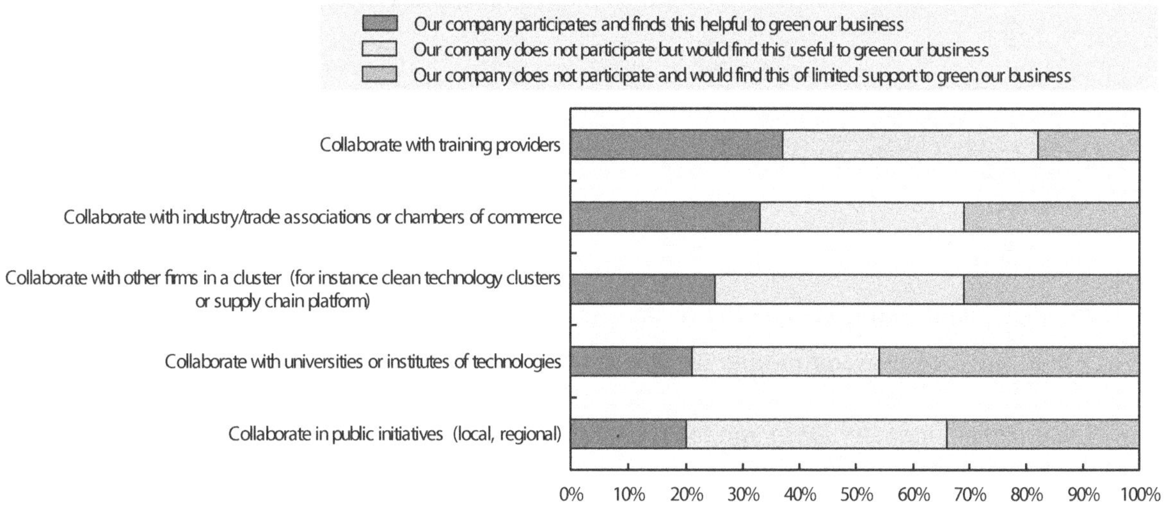

Source: OECD LEED company survey.

Figure 4.8. **Training providers**

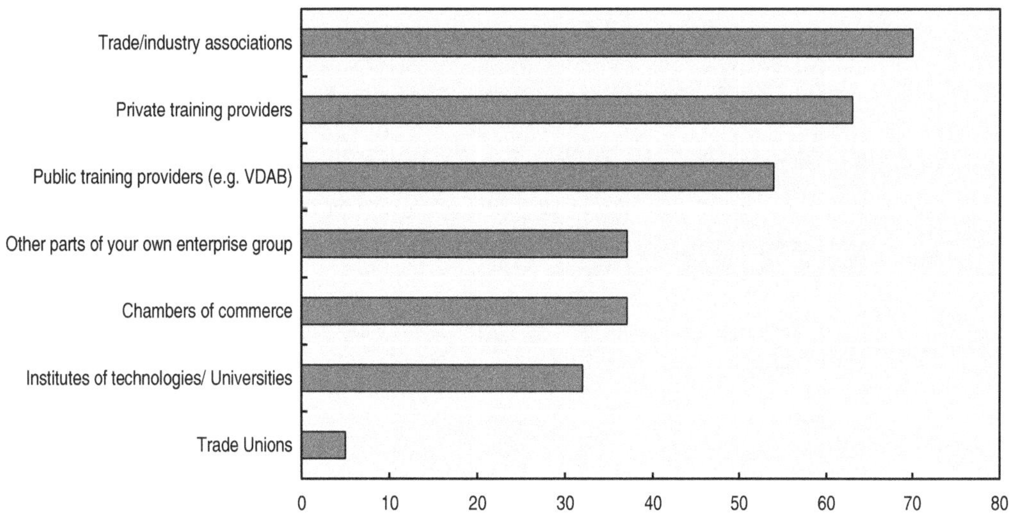

Source: OECD LEED company survey.

In the interviews, on-the-job and in-house trainings by employees were mentioned as the main strategy to improve green skills. The advantages are the match between the training and the skills needs in the firms and the fact that it is done during the working hours.

There are obstacles to the training for the green economy transition. The main obstacles mentioned in the survey are the cost of training (63%) and the timing of the training (60%). The timing presumably mainly relates to the opportunity cost: the time that is spent participating in training is not spent for core tasks. This is mainly a problem for small companies, for whom it may be hard to replace a certain employees for two days of training.

If the cost is perceived as an obstacle for all respondents, some differences exist across sectors. Firms in construction also indicate they do not have enough information on training available in their regions, while firms in the chemical industry say that the training they need doesn't exist in the area.

Table 4.2. **Perceived main obstacles to training**

As a percentage of the total number of firms in the sector

	Lack of information on available training	Cost of training	Timing of possible training	The training is not available in my region	The training I need does not exist
Agriculture	27	60	67	40	33
Manufacture of food products	55	80	65	40	35
Chemical industry	50	70	60	55	65
Construction	53	50	50	50	37

Source: OECD LEED company survey.

Collaboration with industry and trade associations

A third of the companies in the survey collaborate with industry and trade associations and chambers of commerce. This type of collaboration is particularly high for the chemical industry (45%) and for the agriculture sector (33%). It is notable that more than 40% of firms in this sector wouldn't find this collaboration useful. This collaboration is less developed for the food manufacturing sector that however expresses a strong interest in this strategy.

Figure 4.9. **Collaboration with industry and trade associations**

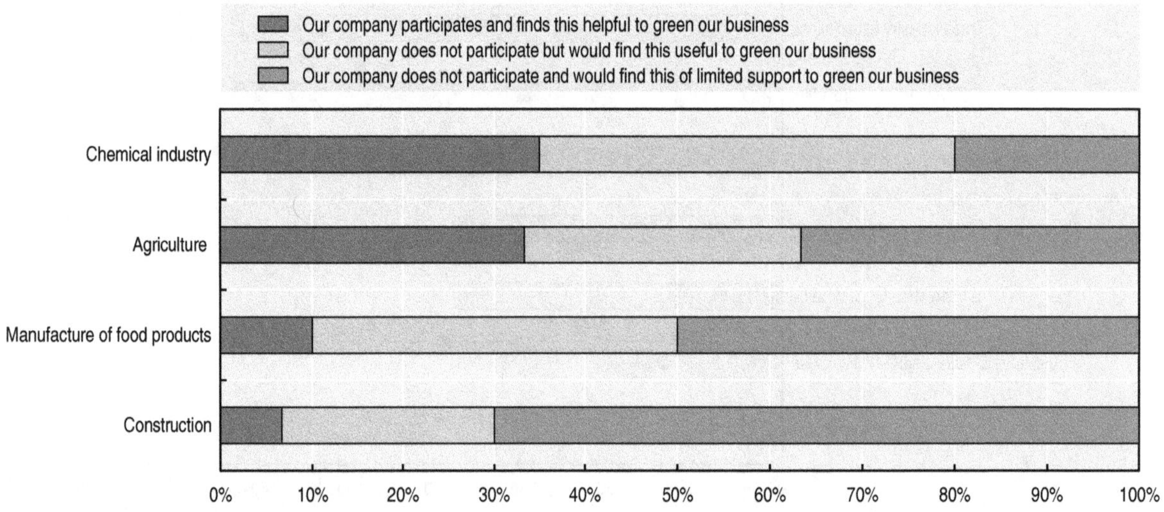

Source: OECD LEED company survey.

Collaboration with clusters or supply chain platforms

A quarter of the firms collaborate with clusters or supply chain platforms and 44% would find that useful. Significant differences exist across industries. In particular firms in food manufacturing and in construction show a very low utilisation rate of this strategy, 5% and 13% respectively. However, firms in food manufacturing seem to believe it would be useful to take part in such platforms in the future.

It is interesting to note that since 2013 the platform that possibly cuts across the value chain most explicitly is in the agro-food sector: the sustainable food transformation project.

Strategies for green skills development

In Flanders, environment related curricula exist but the link between companies and people who have this type of background is not always straightforward. In particular one

Figure 4.10. **Collaboration with clusters or supply chain platforms**

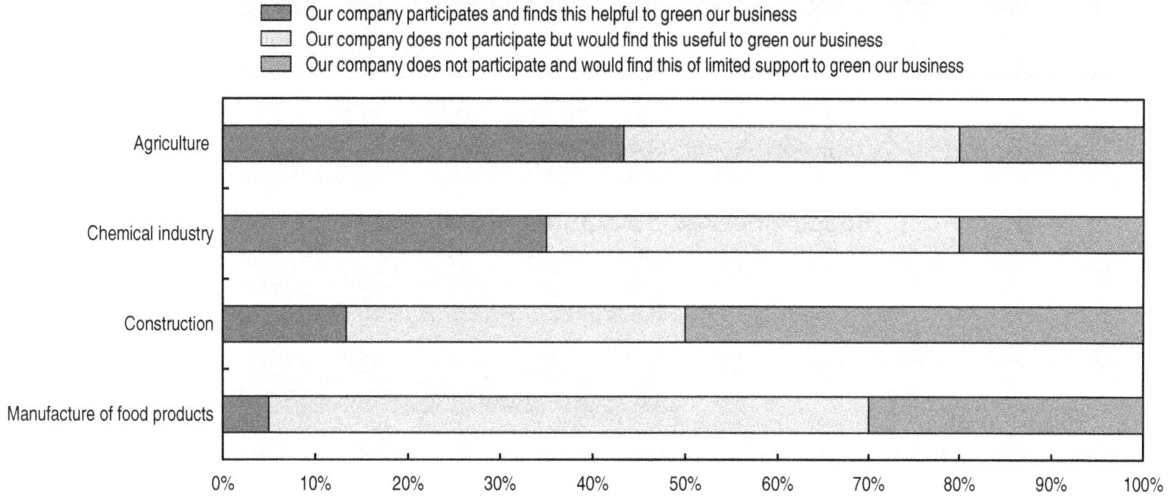

Source: OECD LEED company survey.

issue that was raised during the study is that people with environment-related skills tend to be more critical on company practices and are not always well perceived by firms.

Flemish companies do not expect the education system to create new education programmes on green trends and innovation as the implementation process can be long. Companies that are greening frontrunners also make this comment about the training sector.

Only 21% of the firm collaborate with universities and institutes of technology and a third would find that useful. Interestingly nearly half of the respondents (46%) stated that they wouldn't find this collaboration useful to green their business. The take-up of this strategy is strongest in the chemical sector, which is not surprising, giving the strong focus on technological innovation and the fact that many companies in this sector are large companies.

Figure 4.11. **Collaboration with universities and institutes of technology**

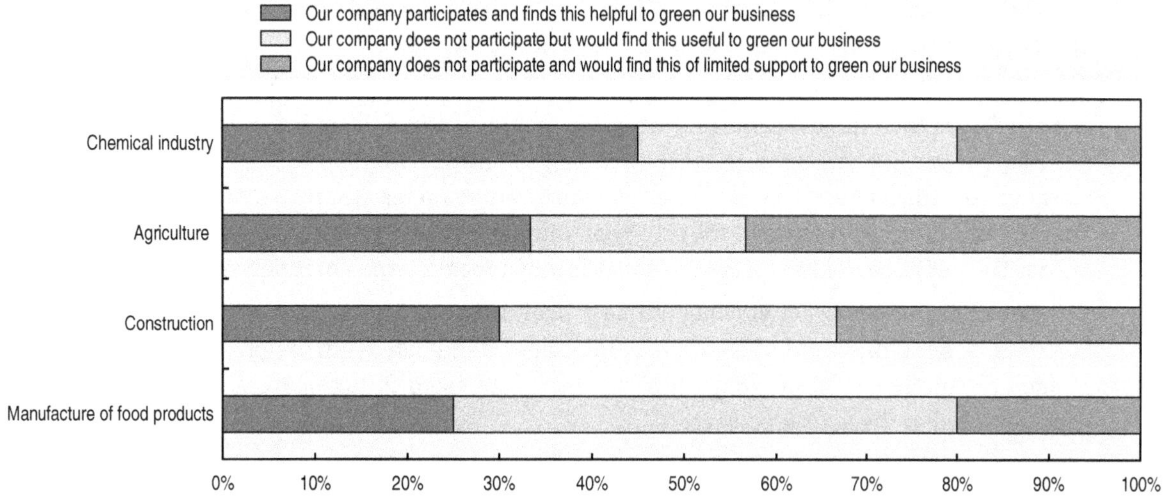

Source: OECD LEED company survey.

Public sector support

Companies can also benefit from public sector support to meet their rising green skills needs. Figure 4.12 below shows that the needs for training provision and subsidies and for greener equipment are the most prominent, followed by employment subsidies, partnership building and consulting. In the interviews, the need for more support for innovation and more support for SMEs in general was also raised.

Figure 4.12. **Support needed from public authorities to green business**

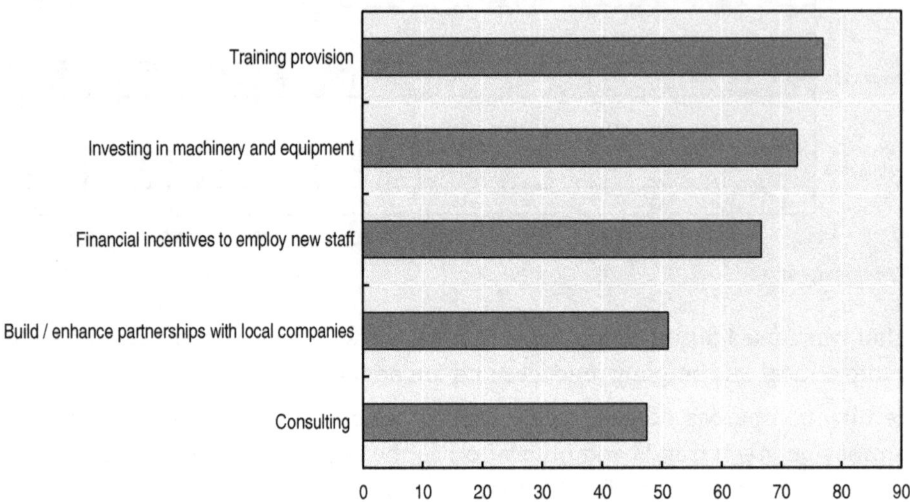

Source: OECD LEED company survey.

Conclusions

Firms play an important role in greening the economy. The survey conducted among companies in Flanders presents information on how business practices and skills needs are changing when firms implement green measures.

The large majority of Flemish companies have taken first steps to green their business especially in relation to waste management and energy efficiency. Among these firms, only a few claim to have completely reshaped their business. This suggests that some of them are not fully aware of the importance of the green transition and others, especially SMEs, do not have enough resources to implement radical changes.

The green transition is having an impact on skills and occupational profiles, and firms signalled that there is an increasing need for technical skills. In order to have the skills necessary to green businesses, more than half of the firms had to upskill or retrain current staff, while a third needed to hire external consultants and less than 10% hired new staff. Training is considered costly and the timing of training courses does not always suit business needs. The public sector is expected to assist firms in meeting the emerging skill needs.

Knowledge-sharing activities could be a useful tool to assist firms in greening their business. Around one third of companies interviewed indicate being involved in this type of activity. Another third of companies would be interested to take part. A large interest was identified in the agro-food sector.

References

Cooke (2015), *OECD LEED "Boosting skills for greener jobs in Flanders", Ghent workshop summary note.*

Ecorys (2010), *Sector Councils on Employment and Skills at EU level: Country reports.*

Essencia (2014), *Acties voor jongeren, www.essenscia.be/nl/acties_voor_jongeren* (accessed 18 December 2014).

Essenscia (2012), *Globaal convenant scheikundige nijverheid en onderwijs: chemie, kunstoffen en life sciences, www.essenscia.be/Upload/Docs/Ondertekende%20onderwijsconvenant%20sector%20chemie.pdf.*

Fevia (2014), *Fevia stelt zich voor, www.fevia.be/#ref=dossier&val=614* (accessed 18 December 2014).

Fisch (2014), *Fisch: ontstaan, www.fi-sch.be/nl/fisch/ontstaan/* (accessed 18 December 2014).

Flanders Food (2014), *Wie is Flanders' Food?, www.flandersfood.com/wie-flanders-food* (accessed 18 December 2014).

IDEA Consult (2011), *Gevolgen van het klimaatbeleid voor de Vlaamse arbeidsmarkt.*

ILO (2011), *Skills for green jobs a global view,* International Labour Organization.

MIRA – AMS (2012), *Transition to a sustainable agro-food system in Flanders: A system analysis.*

OECD (2015), *Aligning Policies for a Low-carbon Economy*, OECD Publishing, Paris, *http://dx.doi.org/10.1787/9789264233294-en.*

STEM Academie (2015), *http://stem-academie.be/* (accessed 15 April 2015).

Tiense Suiker (2015), *www.tiensesuikerraffinaderij.com/nl-BE/Hoe-we-werken/Milieubeleid* (accessed 15 April 2015).

Vlaamse overheid (2014), Globaal convenant scheikundige nijverheid en onderwijs, *www.essenscia.be/Upload/Docs/Ondertekende%20onderwijsconvenant%20sector%20chemie.pdf* (accessed 18 December 2014).

WSE (2011), *Naar een groen arbeidsmarktbeleid:een eerste beleidsverkenning*, Departement Werk en Sociale Economie, Vlaamse Overheid, Depotnummer D/2011/3241/128.

Chapter 5

Policy recommendations

This chapter provides specific advice for developing green skills in local labour markets in Flanders, Belgium. Learnings from the mechanisms used to address green skills challenges in other countries are presented as examples for future policy makers. Specific recommendations for policy makers at the regional (Flanders) level and the local level are presented alongside recommendations for local businesses in order to present the best method of developing green skills in the local area. Adapting education and skills policies and initiatives for the green economy transition.

Recommendation 1.1: Mainstreaming environmental and sustainability principles in all education curricula (activities at school level).

As highlighted in this report, skills for the green economy transition can be defined as "the knowledge, abilities, values and attitudes needed to live in, develop and support a sustainable and resource-efficient society" (Cedefop, 2012). The local roundtables and interviews undertaken as part of this study highlighted the importance of ensuring a generally positive mind-set towards the transition to a green economy amongst all workers. A broad understanding of environmental and sustainability principles should be present in all workers, influencing their expertise, attitudes and skills. Early education of sustainable development could play an important role in raising awareness and shaping attitudes.

Flanders has long been active on environmental education and sustainable development education. For instance, a platform on Education for Sustainable Development with representatives of various policy departments and stakeholders was established to implement the Flemish action plan during the UN decade for Sustainable Development Education (2005-14). However, participants in the roundtables shared their impression that education for sustainability was taking place on an ad-hoc basis rather than systematically.

A systematic approach would require collaboration from a number of different departments and sectors. Therefore, Flemish authorities should continue to collaborate inter-departmentally to build a greater understanding and appreciation of the challenges faced through the transition to a green economy. As noted by the OECD (2013), policy co-ordination between disparate departments, including policymakers responsible for skills development, environmental policy, human resource development and broader economic strategy, can soften the transition to a green economy.

Additional efforts could be made in areas where Flanders performs less well on environmental indicators and where business surveys show limited awareness of green economy considerations (e.g. air quality or water). This could be achieved through dedicated school activities co-ordinated with the STEM academies and organised by specialist bodies such as Vlakwa (Flanders Knowledge Centre for Water). In the Netherlands, for instance, the European Centre of Excellence for Sustainable Water Technology (Wetsus) has developed activities for primary and secondary schools in Leeuwarden in addition to research activities and collaboration with universities (see Box 5.1).

Recommendation 1.2: Mainstreaming environmental and sustainability principles into higher education curricula.

Participants in the roundtables organised as part of this project suggested that sustainability principles should be integrated in higher education curricula to ensure all workers have a broad understanding of environment and sustainability principles. This is particularly relevant for those courses that lead to careers in industries directly impacted by the transition, such as the construction sector, but also for careers in the finance and

Box 5.1. Building a talent pipeline from school to university research: Wetsus, the European Centre of excellence for sustainable water technology

The European Centre of Excellence for Sustainable Water Technology in Leeuwarden has developed a wide range of educational activities to build a talent pipeline for water management technologies. The Centre collaborates with primary and secondary schools working with a team of six teachers on various projects. For primary education, activities revolve around the discovery of water. For secondary education, activities include cluster excursions, design assignments, guest lectures, competitions and the development of teaching materials in collaboration with education.

The Centre has also developed a Master's degree in Water Technology, a two year programme offered jointly by Wageningen University, University Twente and University of Groningen. It also welcomes Ph.D students and post-doctoral researchers and collaborates with a large network of universities.

Source: www.wetsus.nl/.

business sectors. Mainstreaming greens skills into broader curricula can also contribute to increased environmental awareness and enables actors to both drive and adapt to changes associated with the transition to a green economy (OECD, 2013).

Flanders has been active in mainstreaming environmental and sustainability awareness across higher education curricula such as through the Eco-campus project led by the Department of Environment (LNE) in collaboration with the Department of Education. The first eco-campus project (2008-11) had many objectives extra-curricular focuses, including building environmentally sensitive behaviours in student life and on campus. The second Eco-campus project (2011-15) focused more on the adaptation of curricula and providing a platform "to stimulate and support colleges and universities in producing graduates who consider sustainable development and environmental care as the main framework for their professional and private practices".

Future activities should build on the results of the Eco-campus project and continue assisting colleges and universities in the adaptation of curricula especially for business and finance courses. This could also include more activities in partnership, which could contribute towards the development of a future talent pipeline for green sectors.

Recommendation 1.3: Addressing technical skills shortages for the green economy transition.

The firm surveys and interviews with business representatives suggest that technical skills could be a bottleneck with negative impacts on the Flemish transition to a green economy. Flanders has already identified that attracting young people to careers in Sciences, Technology, Engineering and Mathematics (STEM) is of key strategic importance. In 2012, a report by the Flemish Council for Sciences and Innovation highlighted concerns that existing initiatives were not directed to reach a critical mass of pupils/students and teachers. The Flemish government responded with a STEM Action Plan and the Science Communication Plan. In addition, an initiative called STEM platform was launched in 2014, which promotes STEM academies in Flemish municipalities. One quarter of Flemish municipalities now have a STEM academy (e.g. a network of organisations that plan after-school activities around science and technology for children and youngsters up to 18 years old).

The STEM academies could be encouraged to raise awareness of environment education and sustainability as part of their activities. However, policies should not only focus on attracting students in STEM careers through initial education but also explore how to facilitate career pathways into STEM related-sectors through continuing vocational education and training.

Recommendation 1.4: Assist greening industries in building their talent pipeline by further improving the transition from school to work through practical training and skills development.

Transitions from school to work in greener areas of the economy could be made smoother in Flanders. The education system could be made more flexible to quickly adapt to emerging needs connected with the green transition, and collaboration between industry and the education sector should be further intensified through apprenticeship and other work-based training programmes. The Tech partnership in the UK is a good example of how companies and training providers can be mobilised in partnership to deliver greater skills development opportunities in the green sector. This partnership contributes to addressing skills shortages while also helping companies with HR tools boost their attractiveness and strengthen their talent pipeline (see Box 5.2).

Box 5.2. **The Tech Partnership – apprenticeships and HR support to accelerate the flow of talent in the UK tech industries**

The overall objective of the Tech Partnership is to accelerate the growth of the digital economy in the UK. In particular, it aims to inspire young people about technology, accelerate the flow of talented individuals from all backgrounds and help companies develop the technology skills they need for the future.

The Partnership gathers over 500 employers (including top IT firms) and collaborates with universities and colleges to set up apprenticeships. Roughly 30 000 apprenticeship jobs were created in the last 3 years and new tech degrees were developed by employers.

The Tech Partnership provides a wide range of support activities such as skills management tools, Tech ambassadors and HR support. Interestingly, the partnership assisted several small tech firms in redrafting job adverts to attract young talent. This included not only focusing on technical characteristics of vacancies but describing the purpose.

Source: The Tech partnership, *www.thetechpartnership.com/*, presented at OECD LEED Annual forum 2015 Manchester.

In Flanders, on a provincial level, the Regional Technological Centres (whose goal is to facilitate the transition from education to work) could play a more active role in this area. The new Flanders cluster policy could also help to improve talent pipelines in specific sectors (see also recommendation 2.1).

Recommendation 1.5: Continue to support education and training agencies in their efforts to support the green economy transition.

Education and training public agencies such as VDAB (Flemish public employment service), Syntra (Flemish Agency for Entrepreneurial Training) and AHOVOKS (Flemish Agency for Higher education, Adult education, Qualifications and Grants) have well integrated green elements in their activities. The analysis of local initiatives shows that there is a good level of flexibility left to public agencies (in particular to VDAB and Syntra) to adapt their activities to local needs with differentiated programmes in the different Flemish provinces.

Participants in the local roundtables estimated that the collaboration of the various public agencies was rather good and positive. New partnerships should therefore build on, rather than disrupt, existing collaboration. The added-value of the participation of public employment services and agencies in various local projects should be acknowledged and further supported.

Recommendation 1.6: Help develop training for green investors, managers and business leaders and support green entrepreneurship.

The local roundtables in Flanders highlighted the fact that SMEs and entrepreneurs have a critical role to play in boosting green innovation. The OECD survey to businesses indicates that CEO vision is also an important driver for greening company practices. As the survey highlights, CEOs that are convinced of the importance of greening the economy (and that are aware of the opportunities available) can make a big difference in their company directions and support for greening activities. Special attention could be given to "greening" the training provided by business schools and management courses. Training for green investors and green entrepreneurs could be developed with support from public authorities. The certification and training for green investors in Canada (see Box 5.3), the Carbon Trust micro entrepreneur fast track in the UK are good examples of such programmes. In Denmark, a special fund has also been set up to help develop green business models (see Box 5.4).

Box 5.3. **Certification and training for green investors in Canada**

In 2010 the David O'Brien Centre for Sustainable Enterprise in co-operation with Finance and Sustainability Initiative Montreal created the Sustainable Investment Professional Certification (SIPC) Program. This program offers basic sustainability training to business professionals with 70 to 80 hours of self-study curriculum material, online study guidance and certification testing, which culminates in the Sustainable Investment Professional Certificate. The programme is now a part of the John Molson School of Business executive centre.

The SIPC programme is an online sustainable investment certification offered through a business school and it is designed specifically to provide professionals in the finance, investment and corporate world with a practical set of skills and knowledge.

Source: www.concordia.ca/jmsb/programs/executive-centre/sipc.html.

Box 5.4. **The fund for green business development and the accelerator programme for new business models in Denmark**

The Fund for Green Business Development promotes eco-efficiency in Danish firms by giving grants to selected firms. The fund holds around 19 million Euros in the period 2013-16. It supports innovative projects with the potential to create growth and new green jobs in Denmark and act as catalysts for environmental improvements.

The Fund has also joined forces with the Danish Regions and the Regional Municipality of Bornholm to establish an accelerator programme on green business model innovation. The programme was launched in October 2014. The programme recognises as a starting point

Box 5.4. The fund for green business development and the accelerator programme for new business models in Denmark *(cont.)*

that with new business models, "companies can conquer new markets and customer segments as well as increasing their competitiveness". "New business models can work as a catalyst for innovation and they can also lead to significant environmental improvements, e.g. by changing the incentive structure in the market."

The Fund supports businesses in an initial phase to develop an overall business plan. The Danish regions and municipalities assist businesses in a second phase for testing and implementing the new business model.

Source: http://groenomstilling.erhvervsstyrelsen.dk/greenbusinessmodels, http://groenomstilling.erhvervsstyrelsen.dk/greenbusinessfund.

Step up knowledge sharing and partnerships to encourage green innovation

Recommendation 2.1: Increasing knowledge sharing/cluster activities in target sectors and cross sector partnerships.

The company survey highlighted that the chemical industry and the construction sector are advanced in terms of their greening activities, particularly with the support of public agencies and trade associations. Around one quarter of firms interviewed take part in cluster or supply chain platforms to green their business.

The new Flanders innovation policy is likely to reinforce the focus on business cluster policies in relation to the smart specialisation agenda. Clusters are defined as "geographical concentrations of interrelated companies and associated institutions for research, education and training and other supporting institutions, which are active in the same or related domain of value creation." This new policy can be seen as an opportunity to better identify potential skills needs and gaps in selected clusters and tailor the response of education and training providers to business needs.

The OECD (2015) has previously identified inclusive stakeholder management as key to promoting the sustainable use of water and other natural resources. Informal collaboration methods can foster two-way sharing of ideas and technical expertise between stakeholders including layers of government, citizen groups, businesses from diverse sectors and regulators.

The OECD company survey shows that such collaboration is not well spread in the manufacture of food products (only 5% of the firms interviewed). Additional activities should be supported in sectors where a sustainability vision is not yet well developed, but where there is an enthusiasm to do more (e.g. the agro-food sector). These activities could include support for knowledge sharing, road-mapping and joint planning for greening practices. Trade associations could help raise awareness and help launch particular projects during the transition. The development of appropriate communication channels, including web-based technologies when feasible, is a simple method of improving dialogue and information sharing between disparate businesses (OECD, 2015b).

Activities should build on existing structures and replicate good practices from other sectors such as the Academy of the Future project. For instance, the green skills partnership for London used existing networks of employers and colleges to support the development of new forums (see Box 5.5). Beyond sector specific activities, cross-sector and value chain collaborations should be encouraged for instance through broader knowledge sharing platforms or 'innovation theatres'.

Box 5.5. **The London Green Skills partnership**

In 2011, employers, trade unions, education providers, local authorities and community representatives launched the London Green Skills Partnership, a bottom-up initiative with three main objectives: to create local networks to enable stakeholders to work together; to provide training, skills and work experience for locals, including the unemployed; and to transform communities into greener, safer, cleaner and more inclusive places.

The partnership is co-ordinated by Unionlearn, a Trade Union body in charge of education and skills, and includes numerous London colleges (e.g. Lewisham, CONEL, South Thames), employers (e.g. Bovis Lendlease, Lakehouse, Carillion), voluntary sector organisations (e.g. Groundwork), trade unions (UCU, UCATT, UNITE) and Job Centre Plus. The partnership has developed collaborations between training providers, employers, trade unions, the voluntary sector and communities to deliver sustainability training and employment opportunities.

The Partnership includes training for job seekers in both basic and specific environmental skills needed to transform employment into greener jobs in domains as diverse as retrofitting buildings, hairdressing and waste management. Trained individuals also act as "green ambassadors" in their neighbourhoods and workplaces in order to share their green skills with colleagues and neighbours to foster additional change.

Source: www.unionlearn.org.uk/green-skills-partnership, http://erc-online.eu/wp-content/uploads/2014/06/Skills-needs-in-greening-economies_FinalReport.pdf.

Recommendation 2.2: Step up efforts to encourage innovation via platforms for experimentation in order to better link education and innovation and SME support instruments.

The promotion of experimentation within the green economy should be an important dimension of Flanders innovation policy. As previously mentioned, international initiatives such as the "accelerator programme for business models" in Denmark often provide incentives for pilot testing in companies. "Experimentation labs" – places free from rules where students and entrepreneurs experiment, and freely discuss their preferences – are also interesting to the extent that they support experimentation. Examples exist in Ghent (Living Lab) and Eindhoven. Some experimentation labs are fully dedicated to the green economy such as the GreenFabLab in Spain (see Box 5.6).

Box 5.6. **Self-sufficient Fab Lab in Valldaura, Spain**

The Valldaura Labs is a project promoted by the Institute for Advanced Architecture of Catalonia for the creation of a self-sufficient habitat research centre. Located in the Collserola Natural Park, in the heart of the metropolitan area of Barcelona, it has laboratories for the production of energy, food and other products. It develops projects and academic programmes in association with international research centres.

The group comprises three laboratories – Food Lab, Energy Lab and Green FabLab. The laboratories are investigating the processes involved in the production of energy, food and things locally, using the resources of the immediate environment, and developing technologies and knowledge that can be employed in the construction of a new global human habitat.

Source: www.valldaura.net/about/?lang=es.

There are some indications that Flanders is not performing as well as other selected benchmark regions on the promotion of green innovation. This suggests that more emphasis could be placed on instruments that support technology and innovation, such as the initiatives supported by the Institute for Science and Technology (IWT). The example of the German region of Baden Württemberg, which has topped the list of European regions for innovation indicators, shows the importance of dedicated instruments and programmes with public support but also encouraging clusters based on the region's industrial strengths (see Box 5.7).

Box 5.7. **The example of Baden Württemberg (Germany)**

Baden Württemberg has topped the list of European regions for innovation indicators, including green innovation, for many years. The region is said to have the strongest innovative capacity, with no other European region investing as much economic output in research and development.

As the cradle of car manufacturing, the region has built on its industrial backbone to foster innovation in relation to electromobility (fuel cells) and renewable energy. Research in these niches is triggered by public programmes and the funding of strong public research infrastructure (universities, research institutes such as Fraunhofer and Max Planck) as well as by private research by car manufacturers and suppliers. There is a strong relationship between industry and the regional government.

This is facilitated by a clear policy framework with ambitious targets (the environment policy plan) and by public funding. Baden Württemberg is providing €16 million per year to promote climate protection measures. It finances the fuel cells challenge programme as well as the State's electromobility initiative.

Cluster activities are also promoted. The region has created a database of cluster activities and a cluster atlas.

The region is also well connected in European and international networks and hosts a yearly Green Innovation and Investment Forum. The Forum aims to support researchers, start-ups and founders with smart business ideas from the green technology and eco innovation sector from across the continent in collaboration with the European Institute of Innovation and Technology (EIT).

Source: www.isi.fraunhofer.de/isi-wAssets/docs/p/de/vortragsfolien/regionen_cluster/Presentation_Koschatzky.pdf, www.clusterportal-bw.de/, www.green-inno-forum.eu/.

Monitoring the green economy transition: benchmarks and dissemination to inspire local stakeholders

Recommendation 3.1: Support the assessment of the employment impact of the green transition beyond job creation.

When estimating the labour market impact of the transition to a greener economy, policy makers should not only focus on the job creation potential but also on how the transition can help to maintain and secure jobs, for instance by anchoring critical economic industries in local areas. Studies such as the Vlakwa study on the socio-economic importance of water can help raise awareness among business sectors and policy makers of the dependence of local industries on key environmental resources. This is particularly relevant as the OECD company survey highlights that companies are aware of some of the environmental challenges that affect their operation management (e.g. waste and energy) but are less aware of other environmental issues such as water or air quality.

Recommendation 3.2: Provide benchmarks for green economy transition activities at the local level.

Tracking of environmental metrics is important not only to determine the impacts of climate change on existing economic processes, but also to plan for the future impacts of the green transition on labour markets. For example, the monitoring of climate change metrics has enabled the OECD (2015c) to understand the impacts of climate change on the absolute stock and the productivity of natural resources and then calculate the broader impact on economic and socioeconomic outcomes.

The report highlights that limited comparable data is available at the local level. Nevertheless, the project roundtables and final event showed that there is a willingness to provide benchmarks at the local level to encourage and galvanise local actors.

Flanders' regional authorities could assist local areas in their monitoring of the green economy transition. An interesting example is France where a national observatory for employment and jobs in the green economy has been created (see Box 5.8). One of the Observatory's pillars of work is to assist with local indicators in French regional and local areas. It also assists economic sectors to assess the impact of the transition to the green economy.

Box 5.8. **National observatory on green skills and jobs in France**

The Observatory For Green Skills and Jobs (ONEMEV) is a structure for dialogue and work among various stakeholders which is co-ordinated by the French General Commission for Sustainable development. It aims to build a methodological framework to conduct studies, collect data and ensure a shared diagnosis on jobs, professions and training for green growth. It produces an annual review of its activity including a synthesis of the results of observation.

ONEMEV has several working themes. One working theme (workshop 4) gathers regional observatories for training and employment and other local stakeholders to develop methods and tools for collecting comparable regional data.

Source: www.developpement-durable.gouv.fr/L-observatoire-national-des,18551.html.

Recommendation 3.3: Map local initiatives and facilitate the dissemination of lessons from local and international projects.

The report highlights that there is a wealth of initiatives in Flanders related to the transition to a green economy and that provinces and local stakeholders such as Ghent city are taking action and promoting partnerships between education and training providers and businesses. Nevertheless, local initiatives are not always aware of each other. In addition, participants in roundtable discussions identified that there were difficulties with involving businesses.

A mapping of local and sector initiatives would be a first step to avoid the multiplication of platforms. This could help the identification of initiatives that can be replicated or stepped up. This could also increase the visibility of local initiatives, encourage business participation and identify any potential policy gaps to be addressed. In addition, establishing dissemination and exchange mechanisms would help local stakeholders to learn from good practices but also project failures.

Flanders is well integrated in international networks and is involved in a number of initiatives such as the Vanguard project on smart specialisation, or the participation of

Flemish universities and research centres in European Knowledge and Innovation Communities (KIC). The dissemination of international project results and best practices from other countries could be reinforced to inspire local stakeholders. Lessons could be taken from the Green Entrepreneurship Network in Spain (see Box 5.9).

Box 5.9. **The Green Entrepreneurship Network in Spain**

The Red Emprendeverde (Green Entrepreneurship Network) is a platform created to support business creation in green sectors or green-related activities. This network was created by the Fundación Biodiversidad (Biodiversity Foundation), a public foundation of the Spanish Government, depending on the National Ministry of Environment and Rural and Marine Development. The Foundation aims at preserving natural heritage and biodiversity while creating employment, wealth and well-being in the society. The Foundation collaborates with entities and institutions in the public sector, civil society and the business environment.

The Green Entrepreneurship Network seeks to foster entrepreneurship and business growth in sectors or activities related to the environment protection. The Network provides support to entrepreneurs and business owners through 1) drafting or redefining business plans, 2) bringing investors and entrepreneurs together, and 3) providing training and technical assistance. The Network also organizes contests to encourage quality projects while financially supporting some of the most promising initiatives.

Members of the Network include entrepreneurs, investors, or any other actor interested in seizing the economic opportunities arising from the green economy. The Network is co-financed by ESF. The Network benefits of the collaboration of the Spanish Network of Business angels, the Triodos Bank, and the National Innovation Enterprise (ENISA) which is a publicly-financed entity of the National Ministry of Industry, Commerce and Tourism.

The network has been created recently, but already made an important contribution to launching enterprise creation in green economic sectors. The Network brings together over 400 investors and various hundreds of potential entrepreneurs. It has also stimulated the exchange of ideas, created synergies between some of the ideas and also added value to some other projects. The contest has also permitted the identification of some of the most promising projects, and supported their development indirectly (courses, technical assistance, etc.) and directly (grants). Finally, the platform and the communication of this project has contributed to raising awareness of the opportunities emerging from the green economy and encouraging potential entrepreneurs to further develop their ideas in a more structured way.

The network contributed to a clear definition of the terms: green enterprise, green entrepreneur, eco-investor and other stakeholders in the green activities. The on-line platform (*www.redemprendeverde.es*) facilitates the dissemination of good practices to a wider market. The platform also brings investors (venture capitalists, business angels, banks) closer to the ideas (entrepreneurs, businesses) so that it is easier for them to meet and make businesses in a sector of common interest. The platform serves as a social network for entrepreneurs, investors and other actors to exchange and consolidate ideas. It also centralises the services offered by the network (monitoring, technical assistance, training courses, etc.) in a one-stop-shop that is easy to access.

Source: www.redemprendeverde.es.

Next steps for action and implementation

Adapting education and skills policies and initiatives for the green economy transition

OECD Recommendation	Next steps for implementation
1.1 Mainstream environmental and sustainability principles in all education curricula (activities at school level).	• *For regional authorities*: Continue inter-department collaboration for environmental education; provide additional guidance to teachers at school level to address environmental aspects with pupils; provide guidelines as to how STEM academies could integrate environmental aspects; encourage green businesses to organise school visits or participate as 'green ambassadors' at schools; enable public agencies such as the Water centre to participate in raising awareness at schools. • *For local area activities:* Encourage local "green" businesses to participate in extra school curricula activities for instance as "green ambassadors".
1.2 Mainstreaming environmental and sustainability aspects in all education curricula (activities in higher education curricula).	• *For Flanders level public authorities:* Continue to support projects facilitating the mainstreaming of environmental and sustainability aspects in higher education curricula with a more direct focus on the adaptation of curricula, and guidance for trainers. • *For local area activities:* Encourage partnerships and collaboration with universities and business schools to promote the benefits of greening the economy. • *For businesses:* Work with higher education institutions to insist on the importance of environmental aspects.
1.3 Addressing technical skills shortages for the green economy transition.	• *For Flanders level public authorities:* Investigate how to facilitate career transitions into STEM as part of the STEM action plan. • *For local area activities:* Continue contributing to efforts to raise interest in STEM careers. • *For businesses:* Work with the education and training system to ensure that labour market demands are well-articulated and actively feed into programme design and delivery.
1.4 Assisting greening industries in building their talent pipeline: further improving the transition from school to work through practical training.	• *For Flanders level:* Develop stronger labour market information on the regional and local level regarding future industry needs and expected occupations • *For local area activities:* Strengthen outreach and foster partnerships between employers and the education and training system to ensure that supply meets demand. • *For businesses:* Encourage the formation of networks on a sectoral or regional basis to ensure greater transparency in education pathways related to the green economy.
1.5 Continue support for education and training public agencies to work on the green economy transition.	• *For Flanders level:* Continue to support education and training agencies in their effort to embed green activities into their work. Encourage multi-stakeholder approaches and ensure that resources at the local level are devoted to working with other organisations. • *For local area activities:* Promote partnership working and provide platforms to bring local stakeholders together.
1.6 Help develop training for green investors, managers and business leaders and support green entrepreneurship.	• *For Flanders level:* Seek out business leaders who have demonstrated vision towards green activities and promote their efforts to other employers; promote the benefits to SMEs of developing greener products and services. • *For local area activities:* Stimulate local and sector networks among employers to encourage information sharing; work with training organisations to develop specific training for managers. • *For businesses:* Reach out to training organisations to articulate skill needs with respect to the green economy; embed green activities into HR planning and overall business strategies.

Knowledge sharing and partnerships to encourage green innovation

OECD Recommendation	Next steps for implementation
2.1 Increasing knowledge sharing/cluster activities in certain target sectors.	• *For Flanders level:* Support knowledge sharing, road-mapping and joint planning activities for greening practices; target strategic sectors in co-ordination with the Smart Specialisation Strategy. • *For local area activities:* In sectors where a sustainability vision is not yet well developed, but where there is an enthusiasm to do more (e.g. the agro-food sector as identified in the survey), greater support could be provided at the local level. • *For businesses:* Trade associations could help raise awareness and help to launch a transition.
2.2 Step up efforts to encourage green innovation via platforms for experimentation better linking education and innovation and SME support instruments.	• *For Flanders level:* More emphasis could be placed on the transition to a green economy in instruments supporting technology and innovation such as IWT-support. • *For local area activities:* Build on examples from Ghent and promote "experimentation labs": places free from rules where students and entrepreneurs experiment, and freely discuss their preferences; strengthen co-operation with local business and universities.

Monitoring the green economy transition: benchmarks and dissemination to inspire local stakeholders

OECD Recommendation	Next steps for implementation
3.1 Support the assessment of the employment impact of the green transition beyond job creation.	• *For Flanders level:* When estimating the labour market impact of the transition to a greener economy Studies such as the Vlakwa study on the socio-economic importance of water can help raise awareness among business sectors and policy makers as they can highlight the dependence on key environmental resources.
3.2 Provide benchmarks for green economy transition activities at the local level.	• *For Flanders level:* Assist local areas in monitoring the green economy transition by building good local level information and benchmarks to monitor trends over time.
3.3 Mapping local initiatives and facilitating the dissemination of lessons from local and international projects.	• *For Flanders level:* Identify policy innovations at the local level and disseminate evidence on what works in the areas of the green economy. A mapping of local and sector initiatives could help avoid the multiplication of platforms and facilitate business participation. Dissemination mechanisms (e.g. a website, conferences) would encourage greater awareness for local areas. • *For local area activities:* Better report to the regional level both successful initiatives that promote green activities as well as those programmes that have not been optimal to ensure lessons learned are shared across local areas.

References

Cedefop (2012), *Green skills and environmental awareness in vocational education and training*, European Commission, Luxembourg.

Clusterportal Baden Wuerttemberg, *www.clusterportal-bw.de/* (accessed 28 October 2015).

Concordia University (2012), *Sustainable Investment Professional Certification Program www.concordia.ca/jmsb/programs/executive-centre/sipc.html* (accessed 28 October 2015).

European Centre of Excellence for Sustainable Water Technology (2015), *www.wetsus.nl/* (accessed 28 October 2015).

Fundación Biodiversidad, Spain, *www.redemprendeverde.es* (accessed 28 October 2015).

Green Innovation and Investment Forum, European Union, *www.green-inno-forum.eu/* (accessed 28 October 2015).

Groen Omstilling – Green Business Development, *http://groenomstilling.erhvervsstyrelsen.dk/greenbusinessmodels* (accessed 28 October 2015).

ICF GHK (2014), *Skills Needs in Greening Economies.*

Koschatzky, K. (2007), "Methodological framework for cluster analyses", Karlsruhe: Fraunhofer ISI.

L'observatoire national des emplois et métiers de l'économie verte (Onemev), Ministére de L'écologie, du développement durable et de l'énergie, *www.developpement-durable.gouv.fr/L-observatoire-national-des,18551.html* (accessed 28 October 2015).

OECD (2015) *Water and Innovation for Green Growth: Policy Perspectives 2015*, OECD Publications, OECD Publishing, Paris.

OECD (2015b), *Stakeholder Engagement for Inclusive Water Governance,* OECD Studies on Water, OECD Publishing, Paris, *http://dx.doi.org/10.1787/9789264231122-en.*

OECD (2015c), *The Economic Consequences of Climate Change*, OECD Publishing, Paris, *http://dx.doi.org/10.1787/9789264235410-en*

OECD (2013), "Greener Skills and Jobs for a Low-Carbon Future", *OECD Green Growth Papers*, No. 2013/10, OECD Publishing, Paris, *http://dx.doi.org/10.1787/5k3v1dtzlxzq-en.*

The Tech Partnership – Skills for the Digital Economy (2015), *www.thetechpartnership.com/* (accessed 28 October 2015).

Union Learn with the TUC – Green Skills Partnership, *www.unionlearn.org.uk/green-skills-partnership* (accessed 28 October 2015).

Valldaura Labs (2009) – Self Sufficient Labs, *www.valldaura.net/about/?lang=es* (accessed 28 October 2015).

ANNEX 1

Interviewed companies and sector federations

Building sector:

Bostoen nv (Drongen)

Vanhout nv (Geel)

VCB (Vlaamse Confederatie Bouw – Flemish Confederation for the Construction Sector, Brussels)

Chemical sector (including plastics):

Taminco bvba (Ghent)

Ineos Belgium (Zwijndrecht),

Deceuninck nv (Hooglede-Gits) (2 seperate interviews)

Ecosynth (Ostend)

Essenscia (Belgian Federation for Chemistry and Life Sciences Industries, Brussels)

Fisch (Flanders Innovation Hub for Sustainable Chemistry)

Agrofood sector:

Tiense Suiker nv (Tienen)

D'Arta (Ardooie)

FEVIA (Federatie voedingsindustrie vzw, Brussels)

Flemish government:

AHOVOKS (Flemish Agency for Higher education, Adult education, Qualifications and Grants, Brussels)

ANNEX 2

Fact finding roundtables summary note

BOOSTING SKILLS ECOSYSTEMS FOR GREENER JOBS IN FLANDERS

Local roundtables

Antwerp (1st of October 2014)

Roeselare (2nd of October 2014)

Ghent (3rd of October 2014)

This summary note presents key insights of a series of OECD LEED fact finding roundtables on "Boosting skills ecosystems for greener jobs in Flanders". Roundtables were organised from 1st to 3rd October 2014 in Antwerp, Roeselare and Ghent and gathered around 50 participants, including representatives from businesses, trade associations, education and training organisations and public and local authorities.

Antwerp

The roundtable was organised with the support of the Antwerp province. Ludwig Caluwé, Deputy for Economics and International affairs, Province of Antwerp, welcomed participants. Participants started by exchanging experiences of business transitions towards a green economy in Flanders and of perceived obstacles and drivers.

In general, it was perceived that companies lack a vision for sustainability. The current economic crisis makes it less likely for companies to engage in sustainability (some are cancelling prior engagement). Companies do not sufficiently leverage employees' interest in green ambitions, for instance from young employees, in order to accelerate the green transition within their company.

In the building sector, it was mentioned that there was a gap between design (with very ambitious goals) and implementation (business as usual). The process of design should be more integrated with the effective implementation (architects and engineering collaboration). This could require new roles to make connections between various trades, such as a co-ordinator that helps to foster collaboration.

Many initiatives and good practices are ongoing but they are not sufficiently widespread and their results are not sufficiently disseminated.

In terms of the impact on skills and education, there is a shortage of specific technical skills (e.g. bio-engineers) but sustainability and environmental aspects should be covered in all curricula not only in specialised courses. There should be a better link between industry and education. Pilot activities results should be further disseminated. As it is very difficult for education to keep up with the pace of innovation, on-the-job training would also be needed.

Working group 1: Strategies to mainstream sustainability principles in education and training systems and company practices

From initial education to lifelong learning

Encouraging the green economy transition requires a change of attitudes and behaviours towards the environment. This can be facilitated by incorporating sustainability principles in education and training at all levels. At school, such sustainability could be taught alongside other important skills such as engagement, collaboration and listening skills.

The group believed that in Flanders there were already many ongoing initiatives for mainstreaming sustainability. For instance in the building sector, a platform has been developed to allow discussion to anticipate skill needs related to sustainability, and adapt the job profiles for relevant professions. This in turn helps the process of designing specific training programmes for students, unemployed people and on-site workers. The issue is not that the training does not exist, but rather that companies, especially SMEs, choose not to take part in training.

Green in human resource (HR) practices

Green skills or environmental aspects do not appear in Human resources practices and in particular recruitment, which does not help to make them visible as desirable skills for future workers to acquire. Tools to search for green talents and competences could help. At the local level, VDAB activities already support SMEs to help design profiles for job advertisements and tag skills to help job seekers.

"Green talent" would apply to individuals with a specific mindset: creative/innovative, entrepreneurial, but also with community based initiative and the ability to convince. A transition to a green economy would also require leadership skills.

Companies are using corporate social responsibility and their environment practices as a way to build a positive image and attract talents but such green skills core curricula are not always valued in terms of wages. Sometimes, individuals with environment related study are not perceived positively by companies as they could be more critical of company practices.

At a time of economic crisis, job seekers or young people entering the job market are more vulnerable and therefore less likely to criticise company practices or to cherry pick for environmentally minded businesses.

Working group 2: Enhancing integration and value chain thinking

Participants in this group discussed the possibilities to promote value chain thinking as a general attitude in all companies and for all employees.

The group sees a number of existing good practices:

- Recently, new technologies were marketed for extracting valuable resources, such as gold and platinum, from wastewater;
- The Flemish re-use shops ("Kringwinkels") are a good example of a project with a win-win for the environment and (low-skilled) employment;
- 90% of Flemish building waste is being recycled.

However, many challenges remain. Side streams, e.g. from corn production, could be recovered on a larger scale than is the case today. One important barrier is fragmented thinking, whereas integrated thinking should be the mainstream attitude. The Flemish Materials Programme is a good effort of the government to realise more integration thinking, but most government agencies have not taken steps yet, e.g. the lack of integration between energy efficiency and sustainable material use in the Flemish legislation in the construction sector.

Participants believe that education can play a role, but the awareness raising should start at an early age, as is the case with MOS (environmental conservation at school). Professional training initiatives should primarily focus on integration and value chain thinking. On the level of higher education, the Ghent University's integrated platform of master thesis is named as a good example, as is the postgraduate programme on sustainable materials management. However, higher education needs to better bridge the gap between theory and practice.

The group recommended that government pay more attention to communicating good practices, and inspiring and triggering companies to take steps to green their businesses. Local authorities should also lead by example.

Working group 3: Specific needs from SMEs

Participants of this working group started with discussing the effects of the recent economic crisis. On the one hand, SMEs act for survival looking at short horizon and immediate profits. In this context for the majority of SMEs, greening of skills is not their priority. On the other hand, some SMEs see an opportunity to search for new market niches, modify their business model and green their in-company skills. In this case, greening of skills becomes a need to respond to new strategic choices.

An obstacle within the recruitment practice was identified. Namely, SMEs typically have green skills at a low level on their list of requirements. This is magnified by the perception that job-candidates with green skills are perceived to be more expensive and might be more critical of the practices of the SME they would join. In addition, inclusion and searching for green skills amongst job candidates by the human resources departments/recruitment companies is relatively new and not very common.

Another obstacle found was that SMEs typically have limited time and resources available (examples were given from the construction sector), and often cannot keep up with the new technologies and techniques. Further, they may have the willingness amongst the management but not the skills to make strategic changes for greening of skills. Finally, they may have difficulties in following changing policies and increasingly demanding regulations.

The role of the SME's management was found to be very important in enabling the greening of skills. For example, the company management may not have the reflex to do the necessary changes for greening of their business, or the management may not provide the necessary support despite the willingness of employees to engage with greening their skills.

Main conclusions and issues for further discussion

- Senior management in SMEs should better appreciate and recognise the value of employees with green skills.
- SMEs require guidance to green their employees' skills. Specific tools could include financial support and training courses.

- SMEs should be encouraged to let employees take more time to build skills needed for the green transition.
- Adapt practices of human resources departments/recruitment agencies to facilitate the inclusion of green-skills within employee searches.
- Provinces and local government should actively support SMEs on green skills by promoting platforms to exchange: good practices from front-runners and raising citizens' awareness.

West Flanders – Roeselare

The very low unemployment rate of the province of West Flanders is exceptional. The agro-food industry is particularly strong in the region.

Participants started by listing and discussing drivers for companies to green their practices. These include operational costs savings (e.g. limiting waste in the food industry), company policy (seeking a positive image as a means to attract and retain talent although wages and commuting distance are usually the main criteria for workers), "peer pressure" (either from other companies or from individuals within the company) and business opportunities (attracting new clients).

There are a wide range of obstacles preventing companies from greening their businesses. Some obstacles are sometimes overlooked such as supply chain arrangements (in the food industry, for instance, contracts with cleaning companies measured in man-hours rather than performance are contributing to wasting water. This is because the cleaners continue cleaning and using water during the time they were paid for and do not stop after the place is clean).

Training is usually not perceived as a major obstacle. There are different motivations for individuals to choose to train in a topic related to environmental protection.

- When it comes to selecting initial education, the motivations come from a strong personal interest or an idealistic purpose. This may create high expectations from young people entering the labour market and lead to disappointment about what companies offer. The schools/training system could include a more practical component to avoid this disappointment.
- This is the objective for instance of regional technological centres (RTC). This is an initiative of the Flemish government with one RTC per province. The goal of RTCs is to facilitate the transition from education to work (target group: 5th and 6th year students of the secondary technical schools). RTCs support student internships in companies and finance didactic materials/courses that should allow students to acquire experience with machines typically used in a business environment. In West-Flanders, the RTC focuses on a number of industrial sectors (e.g. food industry, transport and logistics, electronics, construction). For each sector, a group of teachers and school managers is brought together to select and evaluate new projects for schools.
- For job seekers or people already employed, the motivation is more pragmatic and associated with jobs available on the market. However, one of the issues is that green skills do not appear prominently in job advertisements.

In terms of skills, the transition to a green economy requires managers to have a basic understanding of sustainability principles and to develop "system thinking". In addition, there is a strong need for technical skills and technical specialists (agriculture engineering, energy technician). Another important aspect is to train workers to work across disciplines or across trades for instance in the construction sector.

A shortage of technical staff (engineers and technicians) has long been identified in the region. This has led to new curricula (eg. specialised masters in new material) and some initiatives to facilitate the transition from schools to companies, for instance with collaboration with schools and children from early age. Some industries have set up "visiting professionals" in schools.

Because of this shortage in the region, industries need to compete to attract and retain talent. The agro-food sector is often perceived as "less attractive". There are shortages for specific functions and skills shortages and mismatch have been identified. Voka (chamber of commerce), UNIZO, universities and colleges collaborated on an awareness campaign to give a positive image of the industry and anchor the sector in the province. This lead to projects such as the "factory of the future, HR-lean management and the Flemish House of food with both company sponsoring and public funding (INTERREG, ESF, and also Flanders funding).

There are already good examples of training offered by public employment services or companies. In the construction sector, VDAB had set up a demonstration building, the "educational house", with practical training on insulation for training employees in the construction sector and also students from secondary schools. The company Bostoen has developed its own technical eco-training. In the agro-food sector, the RTC has developed a one-day training on marine harvest.

There are also examples of knowledge sharing activities between market actors and education providers or along supply chains.

For instance, CONNACT aims to optimise win-win situation along the supply chain by connecting and supporting organisations and companies within and across value chains. CONNACT is involved in the KRAFT project aiming to address shortages in craftspeople, considering not only the needs of highly skilled workers but also disadvantaged groups. *www.connact.be/*.The project organises platform meetings with the supply chain with the main objective of increasing competitiveness.

The Academy of the future project helped address skills needs in the blue energy sector (offshore wind energy parks). In 2013, a lack of technical employees was identified for the sector. The academy of the future helped to map demand and supply with input from the Flanders' maritime cluster (FMC), an interest group of large and small companies active in marine or maritime business. It was identified that workers would require specific skills: language (English or German), technical, autonomy and health and safety. A new professional profile linked to offshore wind (e.g. welding for windmills) was created. The Academy collaborated with Syntra west and university colleges as well as with private trainers. Training will start next April-May 2015 provided the overarching policy framework promoting off-shore wind (Plan Stevin) is implemented.

Main conclusions and recommendations

- Assist companies in creating a vision for greening their business. This could entail funding or support for "road-mapping" activities in specific sectors, support for knowledge sharing among supply chains or cluster activities, as well as specific training for managers and leaders.
- Mainstream sustainability in curricula across the education system.

- Facilitate the transition from school and education to working life with more practical training.
- Make the education system more flexible to adapt for short-terms needs for the green transition. This entails more dialogue between the education system and businesses.
- Ensure a coherent policy framework (incentives and regulation) to drive companies towards greener practices.
- Disseminate and replicate good practices such as the academy of the future and the LED network (*www.lednetwerk.be*).

Ghent

A representative from the Ghent municipality welcomed participants and presented the city's commitment to sustainability. Ghent is the capital and largest city of the East Flanders province with about 250 000 inhabitants. The city is particularly engaged in the transition towards a greener economy. It introduced an action plan for sustainability – "Ghent 2020" – in 2008 and was the first Flemish city to sign the European "Covenant of Mayors" in 2009 with the objective of reducing local CO_2 emissions by at least 20% by 2020 compared to 2007. More than 105 actions and projects are foreseen until 2020. A sustainable procurement strategy is integrated into this action plan. The city is also preparing a new Climate Plan with the objective of becoming carbon neutral and inspiring other cities.

Working group 1: The role of employment and education systems to boost skills for greener jobs

The group discussed that the role of education would be to build awareness at an early stage (school). For now, this is left to individual teachers and initiatives. Training the teachers would help. Other initiatives like eco-campus could help set the example within the education sector. The process of modifying habits is slow.

On the employment services side, VDAB had pilot initiatives on sustainable construction (techniques and skills) mainly targeted at the unemployed to help them retrain. AHOVOKS also helped to define job profiles in the national qualification system linked with the European qualification framework EQF. Some job profiles are being modified to include green awareness skills. Most schools are advanced in adapting curricula based on learning outcomes.

There are good examples of business and education collaboration such as the KIC (Knowledge and Innovation Communities – EU project). The University of Ghent is part of the proposal to run a KIC on raw material. This would link research and companies, help create a new master programme and integrate an entrepreneurship and innovation dimension.

One problem for the education sector is to anticipate skills needs (this can be done with steering committees involving sectors, companies).

There is a perceived lack of collaboration between universities and businesses. The problem of partnerships is that cities/regions and universities are also "competing" to attract talent and investments. Some funded projects (like ESF) imply sharing results. This is at odds with companies' policies to retain commercially sensitive knowledge. At university level, collaboration in projects involves a lot of administrative burden (accreditation process, reporting) – which forces staff to reallocate time away from research to carry out these tasks.

With regard to collaboration and partnerships, the group agreed that no extra structure should be set up as this could entail more administrative burdens. There is also an issue of demonstrating the performance and added value of partnerships as financial resources for partnerships are becoming scarce.

More room should be left for pilots and demonstrations and dissemination activities for good practices should be scaled up.

Main conclusions and recommendations

- Facilitate the collaboration of education institutions with businesses in a flexible way – leave time but fewer rules (reporting, burden).
- Integrate sustainability aspects in all curricula.
- Support student initiatives for greening.
- Disseminate further good examples.
- Create a platform for experimentation between education and businesses: "experimentation labs" free from rules.

Working group 2: enhancing integration and value chain thinking

Participants in this group emphasized the role of more product chain integration. From the first step of extraction of raw materials, production, consumption and recycling, all stakeholders should keep in mind the activities that follow later in the value chain. A value chain approach should be an overall attitude common to employees and managers alike, but that is yet to be achieved. One example is the energy performance certificate for buildings: it covers only one aspect of the green economy and more integration is needed.

The education system is perceived to be slow to respond to new trends. Nevertheless, more programmes should embrace the concept of sustainable design of products. More from private training initiatives could be promoted, although they are rather expensive.

It was noted that employees in the green economy require a different attitude in addition to specific new skills. Employees should be able to leave their comfort zone, be creative and think in an integrated and value chain-oriented way.

Such skills are not only needed in companies but also at the government level since an increasing number of agencies and government bodies are involved in green policy developments.

Four recommendations were formulated throughout this working group as follows:

- Design a sustainability certification for contractors, particularly in the construction sector. Such a label could focus on the company's energy performance or a wider selection of indicators.
- Promote inter-sector internships programmes inside companies. This could stimulate integrated thinking by allowing students to engage with more than one sector.
- Foster innovation and creative thinking in the public sector by acting as an intermediary between different business sectors or between the education and training sector and companies.

Working group 3: Special support from SMEs

Participants of this working group focused on discussing the differences between SMEs that are innovators and early adopters in green skills, SMEs who are beginning to realise the opportunities and those who have not started yet.

In frontrunner SMEs, employees are highly aware and driven by green ambitions. Their green skills usually extend beyond specialised technical skills but also include strong social and communication skills. This is because different skills are required in the company to achieve their green goals. The challenge in greening skills for SMEs is to find the balance between specialised technical skills and inter-personal skills. The educational system should address both and also facilitate wider cross-sector communication.

It is usually up to senior management in SMEs to make strategic choices to green the skills of their employees.

SMEs are facing a range of diverse challenges, including the economic recession, changing policies and demanding regulations, and may lack the time, know-how and finances to invest in greening of skills. Therefore, stimulus is needed from available external support and tools.

Main conclusions and recommendations

- The education system should co-operate with SMEs to understand their needs and expectations, thus ensuring future employees are better suited to the demands of employers with respect to green skills.
- Ensure the education system is adaptable and responsive to enable the development of cross-sector and cross-trade skills, including social and communication skills.
- Use the experience of the front runners in understanding needs and drivers for greening of skills.

Table 3. **Roundtable participant list**

First name	Last name	Organisation
Kathleen	Art	POM Antwerpen
Leen	Audenaert	Departement Leefmilieu, Natuur en Energie
Kris	Bachus	KU Leuven
Janis	Baeten	UGent1010
Adinda	Baro	Dienst Economie – Stad Gent
Veerle	Breemeersch	Academie voor de Toekomst/Syntra West
Joke	Calcoen	LED Ecotechnology
Nathalie	Cliquot	OECD
Pascal	de Meyer	Provincie Oost-Vlaanderen
Yleni	De Neve	LNE
Deira	De Rijcke	UGent1010
Inge	De Saedeleir	SYNTRA Vlaanderen
Gitte	de Vries	Dienst economie en Internationale samenwerking
Jeroen	De Waegemaeker	Instituut voor Landbouw en Visserijonderzoek (ILVO) – Landbouw en Maatschappij
Patrick	Decolvenaer	VDAB Hamme
Joos	Dewulf	Aclagro NV
Gijs	Du Laing	Universiteit Gent
Koen	Eyskens	Dienst Landbouw en Platteland
Peter	Garré	Bopro NV
Frank	Geerts	BuildChem
Michael	Gijsegom	Sam-Co

Table 3. **Roundtable participant list** *(cont.)*

First name	Last name	Organisation
Kenneth	Goedertier	Fonds voor Vakopleiding in de Bouwnijverheid
Barbara	Govaert	Milieudienst Stad Gent
Dirk	Halet	Vlakwa
Heidi	Hanssens	POM West-Vlaanderen
Angela	Hardt	Kamp C Duurzaam Bouwen
Bart	Janssens	Architects in Motion
Irena	Kondratenko	Passiefhuisplatform vzw
Luc	Mentens	ABMB
Fanny	Mestdagh	Stad Gent
andré	raemdonck	SERR/RESOC
Thierry	Semey	Confederatie Bouw Oost-Vlaanderen
Nico	Van Damme	VDAB
Nico	Van Damme	VDAB
Frédéric	Van den Abbeele	UGent1010
Peter-Paul	Van den Berg	Kamp C Duurzaam Bouwen
Dietrich	Van der Weken	i-Cleantech Vlaanderen
Carine	Van Hove	Vito
Willem	Van Peer	fvb ffc Constructiv
Felix	van Roost	Dienst economie en Internationale samenwerking
Wim	Van Stappen	Syntra Midden-Vlaanderen
Johan	Vandebuerie	Dakplus
Johny	Vandekerckhove	VDAB
Daan	Vander Steene	Dienst Economie – Stad Gent
Dirk	Vanderstede	Vlakwa
Alien	Vanhee	Stad Gent
Brecht	Vanlerberghe	Bio Base Europe Pilot Plant
Karen	Verplancke	Boerenbond
Saskia	Walraedt	Essenscia
Tim	Zijlmans	UGent1010

ANNEX 3

Dashboard indicators for Flanders

Theme	Indicators	Value	Level of analysis	Year of analysis
The socio-economic context and characteristics of growth	GDP per capita (US Dollar)	40 014	Regional	2011
	Labour productivity (US Dollar)	70 459	Regional	2010
	Unemployment rate	5%	Regional	2013
	Youth unemployment rate	16.6%	Regional	2013
The environmental and resource productivity of the economy	CO_2 emissions per capita (tonnes)	12.9	Regional	2008
	Volume of municipal waste per capita (hundreds of kilograms)	4.9	Regional	2008
The natural asset base	Renewable freshwater resources per capita (1 000 m^3)	1.8	National	Latest year available
	Water abstraction as % of renewable resources	31.2	National	Latest year available
The environmental dimension of quality of life	Air pollution, level of PM2.5 (micrograms per cubic metres)	17.2	Regional	2013
	Sewage treatment connection rates as % of population	73%	National	2009
Economic opportunities and policy responses	Total R&D expenditure as percentage of GDP	2.4%	Regional	2011
	Government R&D budgets for energy and the environment (as % of total R&D budget)	4.5	National	2013
	Patent applications in green technologies	28.4	Regional	2007
	Trends in employment in sectors producing environmental goods and services (as % of total employment)	0.57%	National	2008-11
	Total environmentally related taxes and labour tax revenue as % of GDP	Total: 2.4% Labour: 14.5%	National	2012

ANNEX 4

Company survey questionnaire

Part I – Company features

1. How many employees work for your company?
   - 3 or less
   - Between 4 and 9
   - Between 10 and 49
   - Between 50 and 250
   - More than 250
2. Which sector do you work in?
   - Agriculture (Crop and animal production and related services)
   - Manufacture of food products
   - Chemical industry
   - Construction
3. What would you define as the area of operation of your company? (You may tick more than 1 box)
   - Local (uw gemeente en omstreken)
   - Regional (Vlaanderen)
   - National (België)
   - International (EU, wereldwijd)
4. In which province is your company located?
   - Antwerpen
   - Oost-Vlaanderen
   - West-Vlaanderen

Part II – Are local industries greening their production and consumption activities?

5. In your opinion, what are the 3 most prominent environmental challenges related to your business and what type of challenges they represent for your company?
   - Energy use
   - Water use and water quality

- Waste management
- Raw Material efficiency
- Air quality
- Biodiversity (for instance nature conservation and protected species)

6. Are you incorporating green measures in your business practices today?

   This includes the development of products, services and processes to address environmental challenges.

   - YES
   - NO

   (If question 6 = "yes")

7. If yes, how would you assess the percentage of your business activities that incorporates green measures

   (If question 6 = "yes")

8. Which environmental challenges do these green measures relate to? (You may choose more than 1 box)

   - Energy efficiency and renewable energy
   - Waste management (waste reduction, recycling)
   - Water efficiency and water quality
   - Pollution reduction (air quality, hazardous chemicals)
   - Nature conservation

   (If question 6 = "yes")

9a. To what degree did the following influence your company to take such measures?

   (If question 6 = "no")

9b. To what degree would the following influence your company to take such measures?

   From a scale of 0 "no influence" to 4 "very strong influence"

	0	1	2	3	4
In line with the company's values, corporate social responsibility					
Director/CEO vision					
Strategic: they create new business opportunities					
Positive for the general image of the company					
Saving operational costs					
Consumer demand					
Pressure by NGOs, neighbourhood, local governments or labour unions					
Regulation compliance					

10. In the past 3 years, would you say you have increased the level of green measures in your company?

    - Yes, I have implemented a small number of green measures
    - Yes, I have implemented a lot more green measures
    - Yes, I have completely reshaped my business to incorporate green measures
    - No

11. What are the main obstacles for the implementation of green measures in your business (multiple choice possible)?
    - ❖ Lack of awareness/information on possible green measure
    - ❖ Lack of consumer demand
    - ❖ Administrative/legal barriers
    - ❖ Lack of knowledge/qualification amongst workers
    - ❖ Lack of innovation
    - ❖ Lack of partnerships opportunities (e.g. industry clusters)
    - ❖ High cost/Lack of financing

Part III – How are jobs profiles and skills needs chaining to adapt to the new transition?

(If question 6 = "yes")

12. If you are implementing additional green measures in your sector, have you had to:

1. Hire additional employees:	Yes ☐	No ☐	Don't know ☐
2. Up-skill or retrain current employees:	Yes ☐	No ☐	Don't know ☐
3. Hire consultancy services:	Yes ☐	No ☐	Don't know ☐

(If question 6 = "no")

13. If you were to implement additional green measures in your sector, do you think you would need to:

1. Hire additional employees:	Yes ☐	No ☐	Don't know ☐
2. Up-skill or retrain current employees:	Yes ☐	No ☐	Don't know ☐
3. Hire consultancy services:	Yes ☐	No ☐	Don't know ☐

14. If you were to recruit or up-skill new/existing employees to implement green measures, to which type of job profiles would these employee belong? (More than one answers possible)
    - ❖ Managers and senior officials
    - ❖ Professional and technical occupations
    - ❖ Administrative, legal and clerical occupations
    - ❖ Sales and customer service occupations
15. What type of skills would you expect are needed from new or current employees to implement more green measures? (More than one answers possible)
    - ❖ Entrepreneurial skills
    - ❖ Knowledge of foreign languages
    - ❖ Legal skills
    - ❖ Technical skills
    - ❖ Managerial skills
    - ❖ Communication and interpersonal skills
    - ❖ ICT

Part IV – Is the education and employment system appropriate to face these changes?

(If question 12.2 = "yes")

16. If you have offered training to your employees to implement additional green measures products and services in your firm, what type of training have you offered?

    1. On-the-job training (training during working hours)? Yes ☐ No ☐
    2. Off-the-job (training away from the individuals immediate work position, whether on your premises or elsewhere) Yes ☐ No ☐

(If question 12.2 = "no" or question 6 = "no")

16a. If you were to offer training to your employees to implement additional green measures products and services in your firm, what type of training have/would you offer?

    1. On-the-job training (training during working hours) Yes ☐ No ☐
    2. Off-the-job (training away from the individuals immediate work position, whether on your premises or elsewhere) Yes ☐ No ☐

17. Which type of training providers have you or would you be likely to use?
    - Trade/industry associations
    - Chambers of commerce
    - Institutes of technologies/ Universities
    - Private training providers
    - Public training providers (e.g. VDAB)
    - Other parts of your own enterprise group
    - Trade Unions
18. Is it important that?
    - The training is delivered by accredited trainers Yes ☐ No ☐
    - Providing formal (nationally recognised) qualifications Yes ☐ No ☐
19. What do you think could be main difficulties in relation to training? (You can tick more than one)
    - Lack of information on available training
    - Cost of training
    - Timing of possible training
    - The training is not available in my region
    - The training I need does not exist
20. If you decided to upskill/train your staff regarding green measures, how long do you think it would take between your decision and the actual delivery of the training/upskilling?
    - Less than 1 week
    - 1 week to 1 month
    - Between 1 and 3 months
    - Between 3 and 6 months
    - Between 6 months and one year
    - More than one year

Part V - The support role of public sector and knowledge sharing

21. Which of the following activities are you involved in and/or would you find helpful to assist you in greening your business?

	Our company participates and finds this helpful to green our business	Our company does not participate but would find this useful to green our business	Our company does not participate and would find this of limited support to green our business
Collaborate with other firms in a cluster (for instance clean technology clusters or supply chain platform)			
Collaborate with industry/trade associations or chambers of commerce			
Collaborate with universities or institutes of technologies			
Collaborate with training providers			
Collaborate in public initiatives (local, regional)			

22. To what extent would you need support from public authorities for the following activities with the objective to green your business?

From a scale from 0 ="I do not need support" to 5 = "Support is crucial"

	0	1	2	3	4	5
Training activities						
Consulting (e.g. regarding markets, technological processes, estimation of potential, competitive analysis and trends)						
Financial incentives to employ new staff						
Build/enhance partnerships with local companies, scientists and entrepreneurs						
Investing in machinery and equipment						

ORGANISATION FOR ECONOMIC CO-OPERATION AND DEVELOPMENT

The OECD is a unique forum where governments work together to address the economic, social and environmental challenges of globalisation. The OECD is also at the forefront of efforts to understand and to help governments respond to new developments and concerns, such as corporate governance, the information economy and the challenges of an ageing population. The Organisation provides a setting where governments can compare policy experiences, seek answers to common problems, identify good practice and work to co-ordinate domestic and international policies.

The OECD member countries are: Australia, Austria, Belgium, Canada, Chile, the Czech Republic, Denmark, Estonia, Finland, France, Germany, Greece, Hungary, Iceland, Ireland, Israel, Italy, Japan, Korea, Latvia, Luxembourg, Mexico, the Netherlands, New Zealand, Norway, Poland, Portugal, the Slovak Republic, Slovenia, Spain, Sweden, Switzerland, Turkey, the United Kingdom and the United States. The European Union takes part in the work of the OECD.

OECD Publishing disseminates widely the results of the Organisation's statistics gathering and research on economic, social and environmental issues, as well as the conventions, guidelines and standards agreed by its members.

LOCAL ECONOMIC AND EMPLOYMENT DEVELOPMENT (LEED)

The OECD Programme on Local Economic and Employment Development (LEED) has advised governments and communities since 1982 on how to respond to economic change and tackle complex problems in a fast-changing world. Its mission is to contribute to the creation of more and better quality jobs through more effective policy implementation, innovative practices, stronger capacities and integrated strategies at the local level. LEED draws on a comparative analysis of experience from the five continents in fostering economic growth, employment and inclusion. For more information on the LEED Programme, please visit *www.oecd.org/cfe/leed*.

OECD PUBLISHING, 2, rue André-Pascal, 75775 PARIS CEDEX 16
(84 2016 08 1 P) ISBN 978-92-64-26525-7 – 2017

www.ingramcontent.com/pod-product-compliance
Lightning Source LLC
LaVergne TN
LVHW081411110826
845149LV00010B/1710

* 9 7 8 9 2 6 4 2 6 5 2 5 7 *